Green Mountain Grill Davy Crockett Grill/Smoker Cookbook

Enjoy 120 Easy Tasty Grilled Recipes for Your Green Mountain Grill

By David Handsome

Warning-Disclaimer

The purpose of this book is to educate and entertain. The author or publisher does not guarantee that anyone following the techniques, suggestions, tips, ideas, or strategies will become successful. The author and publisher shall have neither liability or responsibility to anyone with respect to any loss or damage caused, or alleged to be caused, directly or indirectly by the information contained in this book.

TABLE OF CONTENTS

Introduction..9

CHAPTER 1..10

Beef Recipes 10

Grilled and pulled beef...10
Grilled beef jerky..10
Reverse Seared Flank Steak..11
Grilled Midnight Brisket...12
Grilled Butter Basted Porterhouse Steak...................13
Cocoa Crusted Grilled Flank steak............................13
Green Mountain Grill Prime Rib Roast........................14
Grilled Longhorn Cowboy Tri-Tip................................15
Green Mountain Grill Teriyaki Beef Jerky...................15
Grilled Butter Basted Rib-eye.....................................16
Grilled Brisket...17
Grilled Ribeye Steaks..18
Grilled Trip tip with java Chophouse..........................18
Supper Beef Roast...19
Green Mountain Grill Deli-style Roast beef................19

CHAPTER 2..21

Pork Recipes 21

Simple Grilled Pork ribs...21
Roasted Pork with Balsamic Strawberry Sauce.........21
Green Mountain Grill pork crown Roast......................22
Wet-Rubbed St. Louis Ribs...23
Cocoa Crusted Pork Tenderloin..................................24
Grilled Bacon..24
Grilled pork Chops..25
Wood pellet Blackened Pork Chops............................26
Teriyaki Pineapple Pork Tenderloin Sliders................26
Grilled Tenderloin with fresh herb sauce....................27

Grilled shredded pork tacos············28
Wood Pellet Togarashi Pork tenderloin·············28
Wood Pellet Pulled Pork·············29
Grilled Pork Ribs·············30
Grilled Spicy Candied Bacon·············30

CHAPTER 3·············32

Lamb Recipes·············32

Grilled Lamb chops·············32
Grilled Lamb Shoulder·············32
Grilled Pulled Lamb Sliders·············33
Grilled Lamb Meatballs·············34
Crown Rack of lamb·············35
Grilled Leg of Lamb·············36
Grilled Aussie Leg of Lamb Roast·············36
Simple Grilled Lamb Chops·············37
Grilled Lamb with Brown Sugar Glaze·············38
Grilled leg of lambs Steaks·············39
Grilled Lamb Loin Chops·············39
Spicy Chinese Cumin Lamb Skewers·············40
Green Mountain Grill Dale's Lamb·············41
Garlic and Rosemary Grilled Lamb Chops·············42
Grilled LambChops·············42

CHAPTER 4·············44

Poultry Recipes·············44

Grilled Chicken Kabobs·············44
Grilled Chicken·············45
Wood pellet chicken breasts·············45
Grilled Spatchcock Turkey·············46
Grilled Cornish Hens·············47
Grilled and fried chicken wings·············47
Grilled Buffalo Chicken Leg·············48
Wood Pellet Chile Lime Chicken·············48
Wood pellet Sheet pan Chicken Fajitas·············49

Buffalo Chicken Flatbread..50
Grilled Buffalo Chicken 50
Beer Can Chicken...51
Wood pellet Chicken wings with spicy Miso.....................52
Barbecue Chicken wings 52
Bacon-wrapped Chicken Tenders..53
CHAPTER 5...55
Vegan and vegetarian Recipes..55
Grilled Mushrooms...55
Grilled Zucchini Squash Spears..55
Whole Roasted Cauliflower with Garlic Parmesan Butter....56
Wood Pellet Cold Grilled Cheese...57
Grilled Asparagus and Honey Glazed Carrots....................57
Grilled Deviled Eggs...58
Grilled Vegetables..59
Grilled Asparagus..59
Grilled Acorn Squash... 60
Vegan Grilled Carrot Dogs..61
Grilled Vegetables..61
Wood Pellet Grill Spicy Sweet Potatoes...........................62
Grilled Stuffed Zucchini 63
Grilled Mexican Street Corn...64
Wood Pellet Bacon Wrapped Jalapeno Poppers................65
CHAPTER 6...66
Fish and Seafood..66
Grilled salmon...66
Wood Pellet Teriyaki Grilled Shrimp.................................. 66
Grilled Scallops..67
Grilled Shrimp Scampi...68
Grilled Buffalo Shrimp...68
Grilled Salmon Sandwich..69
Grilled Teriyaki salmon..70
Wood Pellet Togarashi Grilled Salmon...............................71

Grilled Lingcod..71

Wood pellet Rockfish...72

Wood Pellet Salt and Pepper Spot Prawn Skewers.............. 72

Bacon-wrapped Shrimp.. 73

Bacon-wrapped Scallops...74

Grilled Lobster Tail...74

Wood Pellet Garlic Dill Grilled Salmon.............................75

CHAPTER 7..77

Side dishes..77

Grilled Carrots..77

Grilled Brussels Sprouts..77

Wood pellet Spicy Brisket..78

Pellet Grill Funeral Potatoes..79

Smoky Caramelized Onions on the Pellet Grill................. 80

Hickory Grilled Green Beans..80

Grilled Corn on the Cob... 81

Grilled Vegetables...82

Easy Grilled Corn...82

Seasoned Potatoes on Smoker.. 83

CHAPTER 8..84

Cheese, Nuts, Breads and Desserts....................................84

Grilled Pumpkin Pie...84

Pellet-Grill Flatbread Pizza...85

Grilled Nut Mix...86

Grilled Peaches and Cream...86

Green Mountain Grill Chicken Flatbread...........................87

Grilled Homemade Croutons.. 88

Grilled Cheddar Cheese... 88

Grilled Mac and Cheese..89

Berry Cobbler on a pellet grill.. 90

Pellet Grill Apple Crisp...91

CHPTER 9...92

Rub and Sauces recipes··92

    Grilled Tomato Cream Sauce··································92

    Grilled Mushroom Sauce······································93

    Grilled Cranberry Sauce·······································93

    Grilled sriracha sauce···94

    Grilled soy sauce···95

    Grilled Garlic Sauce··95

    Grilled Cherry BBQ Sauce···································96

    Grilled Garlic White Sauce···································97

CHAPTER 11··98

  A healthy 21-day Meal Plan·································98

CONCLUSION···100

APPENDIX: MEASUREMENT CONVERSION TABLE············101

INTRODUCTION

2020 Design, Solved Issues with grill some older models experience. Single Grease Tray. The Davy Crockett is the ultimate portable grill. It comes with a digital WiFi controller (control and monitor through our iOS or Android mobile application), a meat probe, a peaked lid for stand-up chicken/ large fowl/ rib racks, a convenience tray with utensil hooks. Also included is Sense-Mate, a thermal sensor which constantly monitors grill temperature.

It can run on 12V or 120AC so its perfect for home or camping, tail-gating, hunting, house-boating, music festivals or anywhere you can take it. Weighing in at 57 pounds with fold-able legs, it can be placed in the trunk of any car. This Listing includes Includes Pellethead Durable All Weather Cover ($42.95 Value)

This book provides you many mouthwatering recipes for your Green Mountain Grill Davy Crockett Grill/Smoker! Including:

Beef Recipes
Pork Recipes
Lamb Recipes
Poultry Recipes
Vegan and Vegetarian Recipes
Fish and Seafood Recipes
Side dishes
Cheese, Nuts, Breads and Desserts
Rub and Sauces recipes

Now let's move on to your recipe world!

CHAPTER 1

Grilled and pulled beef

What more would you ask for after a beef Grilled on low heat for 5 hours then braised on the stovetop with beer until fork tender?
Prep time: 10 minutes, **Cook time:** 6 hours; **Serves:** 6

Ingredients

- ➢ 4 lb beef sirloin tip roast
- ➢ 1/2 cup bbq rub
- ➢ 2 bottles of amber beer
- ➢ 1 bottle barbecues sauce

Preparation Method

1. Turn your Green Mountain Grill onto smoke setting then trim excess fat from the steak.
2. Coat the steak with bbq rub and let it smoke on the grill for 1 hour.
3. Continue cooking and flipping the steak for the next 3 hours. Transfer the steak to a braising vessel .add the beers.
4. Braise the beef until tender then transfer to a platter reserving 2 cups of cooking liquid.
5. Use a pair of forks to shred the beef and return it to the pan. Add the reserved liquid and barbecue sauce. Stir well and keep warm before serving.
6. Enjoy.

Nutritional Information

Calories 829, Total fat 46g, Saturated fat 18g, Total carbs 4g, Net carbs 4g, Protein 86g, Sugar 0g, Fiber 0g, Sodium: 181mg

Grilled beef jerky

This home-cooked wood pellet beef jerky is so good that it will leave you whipping up batches on the regular.
Prep time: 15 minutes, **Cook time:** 5 hours; **Serves:** 10

Ingredients

- 3 lb sirloin steaks, sliced into 1/4 inch thickness
- 2 cups soy sauce
- 1/2 cup brown sugar
- 1 cup pineapple juice
- 2 tbsp sriracha
- 2 tbsp red pepper flake
- 2 tbsp hoisin
- 2 tbsp onion powder
- 2 tbsp rice wine vinegar
- 2 tbsp garlic, minced

Preparation Method

1. Mix all the ingredients in a ziplock bag. Seal the bag and mix until the beef is well coated. Ensure you get as much air as possible from the ziplock bag.
2. Put the bag in the fridge overnight to let marinate. Remove the bag from the fridge 1 hour prior to cooking.
3. Startup your wood pallet grill and set it to smoke setting. Layout the meat on the grill with half-inch space between them.
4. Let them cook for 5 hours while turning after every 2-1/2 hours.
5. Transfer from the grill and let cool for 30 minutes before serving.
6. enjoy.

Nutritional Information

Calories 80, Total fat 1g, Saturated fat 0g, Total carbs 5g, Net carbs 5g, Protein 14g, Sugar 5g, Fiber 0g, Sodium: 650mg

Reverse Seared Flank Steak

The reverse searing method may sound complicated and fancy but its the easiest. Moreover, it yields juicy, tender, and perfectly cooked beef that will brow you away.
Prep time: 10 minutes, **Cook time:** 10 minutes; **Serves:** 2

Ingredients

- 1.5 lb Flanks steak
- 1 tbsp salt
- 1/2 onion powder
- 1/4 tbsp garlic powder
- 1/2 black pepper, coarsely ground

Preparation Method

1. Preheat your Green Mountain Grill to 225°F.

2. In a mixing bowl, mix salt, onion powder, garlic powder, and pepper. Generously rub the steak with the mixture.
3. Place the steaks on the preheated grill, close the lid, and let the steak cook.
4. Crank up the grill to high then let it heat. The steak should be off the grill and tented with foil to keep it warm.
5. Once the grill is heated up to 450°F, place the steak back and grill for 3 minutes per side.
6. Remove from heat, pat with butter, and serve. Enjoy.

Nutritional Information

Calories 112, Total fat 5g, Saturated fat 2g, Total carbs 1g, Net carbs 1g, Protein 16g, Sugar 0g, Fiber 0g, Sodium: 737mg

Grilled Midnight Brisket

This is an irresistible delicious beef that combines slow cooking with a long braise serving you with a ribbon winner meal.
Prep time: 15 minutes, **Cook time:** 12 hours; **Serves:** 6

Ingredients

1. 1 tbsp Worcestershire sauce
2. 1 tbsp Traeger beef Rub
3. 1 tbsp Traeger Chicken rub
4. 1 tbsp Traeger Blackened Saskatchewan rub
5. 5 lb flat cut brisket
6. 1 cup beef broth

Preparation Method

1. Rub the sauce and rubs in a mixing bowl then rub the mixture on the meat.
2. Preheat your grill to 180°F with the lid closed for 15 minutes. You can use super smoke if you desire.
3. Place the meat on the grill and grill for 6 hours or until the internal temperature reaches 160°F.
4. Remove the meat from the grill and double wrap it with foil.
5. Add beef broth and return to grill with the temperature increased to 225°F. Cook for 4 hours or until the internal temperature reaches 204°F.
6. Remove from grill and let rest for 30 minutes. Serve and enjoy with your favorite BBQ sauce.

Nutritional Information

Calories 200, Total fat 14g, Saturated fat 6g, Total carbs 3g, Net carbs 3g, Protein 14g, Sugar 0g, Fiber 0g, Sodium: 680mg

Grilled Butter Basted Porterhouse Steak

Are you a lover of steak? This awsome steak might be the best steak you ever tasted. It's easy to make and comes out perfectly when you master the art of preparing it.
Prep time: 15 minutes, **Cook time:** 40 minutes; **Serves:** 4

Ingredients

- 4 tbsp butter, melted
- 2 tbsp Worcestershire sauce
- 2 tbsp Dijon mustard
- Traeger Prime rib rub

Preparation Method

1. Set your Green Mountain Grill to 225°F with the lid closed for 15 minutes.
2. In a mixing bowl, mix butter, sauce, dijon mustard until smooth. brush the mixture on the meat then season with the rub.
3. Arrange the meat on the grill grate and cook for 30 minutes.
4. Use tongs to transfer the meat to a patter then increase the heat to high.
5. Return the meat to the grill grate to grill until your desired doneness is achieved.
6. Baste with the butter mixture again if you desire and let rest for 3 minutes before serving. Enjoy.

Nutritional Information

Calories 726, Total fat 62g, Saturated fat 37g, Total carbs 5g, Net carbs 4g, Protein 36g, Sugar 1g, Fiber 1g, Sodium: 97mg, Potassium 608mg

Cocoa Crusted Grilled Flank steak

This ridiculously rich and flavourful steak is a complete and big win if you have invited some guests in your home or want to surprise your family.
Prep time: 15 minutes, **Cook time:** 6 minutes; **Serves:** 7

Ingredients

- 1 tbsp cocoa powder
- 2 tbsp chili powder
- 1 tbsp chipotle chili powder
- 1/2 tbsp garlic powder
- 1/2 tbsp onion powder
- 1-1/2 tbsp brown sugar
- 1 tbsp cumin

- 1 tbsp Grilled paprika
- 1 tbsp kosher salt
- 1/2 tbsp black pepper
- Olive oil
- 4 lb Flank steak

Preparation Method

1. Whisk together cocoa, chili powder, garlic powder, onion powder, sugar, cumin, paprika, salt, and pepper in a mixing bowl.
2. Drizzle the steak with oil then rub with the cocoa mixture on both sides.
3. Preheat your Green Mountain Grill for 15 minutes with the lid closed.
4. Cook the meat on the grill grate for 5 minutes or until the internal temperature reaches 135°F.
5. Remove the meat from the grill and let it cool for 15 minutes to allow the juices to redistribute.
6. Slice the meat against the grain and on a sharp diagonal.
7. Serve and enjoy.

Nutritional Information

Calories 420, Total fat 26g, Saturated fat 8g, Total carbs 21g, Net carbs 13g, Protein 3g, Sugar 7g, Fiber 8g, Sodium: 2410mg

Green Mountain Grill Prime Rib Roast

This is an impressive rib roast with a golden brown skin that is a real crowd-pleaser.
Prep time: 5 minutes, **Cook time:** 4 hours; **Serves:** 10

Ingredients

- 7 lb bone prime rib roast
- Traeger prime rib rub

Preparation Method

1. Coat the roast generously with the rub then wrap in a plastic wrap. let sit in the fridge for 24 hours to marinate.
2. Set the temperatures to 500°F.to to preheat with the lid closed for 15 minutes.
3. Place the rib directly on the grill fat side up and cook for 30 minutes.
4. Reduce the temperature to 300°F and cook for 4 hours or until the internal temperature is 120°F- rare, 130°F-medium rare, 140°F-medium and 150°F-well done.
5. Remove from the grill and let rest for 30 minutes then serve and enjoy.

Nutritional Information

Calories 290, Total fat 23g, Saturated fat 9.3g, Total carbs 0g, Net Carbs 0g, Protein 19g, Sugar 0g, Fiber 0g, Sodium: 54mg, Potassium 275mg

Grilled Longhorn Cowboy Tri-Tip

The ground coffee gives this Grilled longhorn cowboy tri-tip a strong bark to seal all the natural juices. This gives the meat the superb flavors.
Prep time: 15 minutes, **Cook time:** 4 hours; **Serves:** 7

Ingredients

3 lb tri-tip roast
1/8 cup coffee, ground
1/4 cup Traeger beef rub

Preparation Method

1. Preheat the grill to 180°F with the lid closed for 15 minutes.
2. Meanwhile, rub the roast with coffee and beef rub. Place the roast on the grill grate and smoke for 3 hours.
3. Remove the roast from the grill and double wrap it with foil. Increase the temperature to 275°F.
4. Return the meat to the grill and let cook for 90 minutes or until the internal temperature reaches 135°F.
5. Remove from the grill, unwrap it and let rest for 10 minutes before serving.
6. Enjoy.

Nutritional Information

Calories 245, Total fat 14g, Saturated fat 4g, Total Carbs 0g, Net Carbs 0g, Protein 23g, Sugar 0g, Fiber 0g, Sodium: 80mg

Green Mountain Grill Teriyaki Beef Jerky

This is a perfect snack, especially when watching a game or hiking. Teriyaki beef jerky is deliciously smoky, chewy and packed with flavors
Prep time: 15 minutes, **Cook time:** 5 hours; **Serves:** 10

Ingredients

➢ 3 cups soy sauce
➢ 2 cups brown sugar

- ➢ 3 garlic cloves
- ➢ 2-inch ginger knob, peeled and chopped
- ➢ 1 tbsp sesame oil
- ➢ 4 lb beef, skirt steak

Preparation Method

1. Place all the ingredients except the meat in a food processor. Pulse until well mixed.
2. Trim any excess fat from the meat and slice into ¼ inch slices. Add the steak with the marinade into a zip lock bag and let marinate for 12-24 hours in a fridge.
3. Set the Green Mountain Grill to smoke and let preheat for 5 minutes.
4. Arrange the steaks on the grill leaving a space between each. Let smoke for 5 hours.
5. Remove the steak from grill and serve when warm.

Nutritional Information

Calories 80, Total fat 1g, Saturated fat 0g, Total Carbs 7g, Net Carbs 0g, Protein 11g, Sugar 6g, Fiber 0g, Sodium: 390mg

Grilled Butter Basted Rib-eye

Did you just buy a Green Mountain Grill and looking for amazing recipes to try on it? Look no further. This is a delicious butter busted rib-eye is the one you need.
Prep time: 20 minutes, **Cook time:** 20 minutes; **Serves:** 4

Ingredients

- ➢ 2 rib-eye steaks, bone-in
- ➢ Slat to taste
- ➢ Pepper to taste
- ➢ 4 tbsp butter, unsalted

Preparation Method

1. Mix steak, salt, and pepper in a ziplock bag. Seal the bag and mix until the beef is well coated. Ensure you get as much air as possible from the ziplock bag.
2. Set the Green Mountain Grill temperature to high with closed lid for 15 minutes. Place a cast-iron into the grill.
3. Place the steaks on the hottest spot of the grill and cook for 5 minutes with the lid closed.
4. Open the lid and add butter to the skillet. When it's almost melted place the steak on the skillet with the grilled side up.
5. Cook for 5 minutes while busting the meat with butter. Close the lid and cook until the internal temperature is 130°F.

6. Remove the steak from skillet and let rest for 10 minutes before enjoying with the reserved butter.

Nutritional Information

Calories 745, Total fat 65g, Saturated fat 32g, Total Carbs 5g, Net Carbs 5g, Protein 35g, Sugar 0g, Fiber 0g

Grilled Brisket

Taking everyone's favorite brisket and infusing it with wood-fired flavor brings out a mouthwatering dinner meal for you and your family.
Prep time: 20 minutes, **Cook time:** 9 hours; **Serves:** 10

Ingredients

- ➢ 2 tbsp garlic powder
- ➢ 2 tbsp onion powder
- ➢ 2 tbsp paprika
- ➢ 2 tbsp chili powder
- ➢ 1/3 cup salt
- ➢ 1/3 cup black pepper
- ➢ 12 lb whole packer brisket, trimmed
- ➢ 1-1/2 cup beef broth

Preparation Method

1. Set your wood pellet temperature to 225°F. Let preheat for 15 minutes with the lid closed.
2. Meanwhile, mix garlic, onion, paprika, chili, salt, and pepper in a mixing bowl.
3. Season the brisket generously on all sides.
4. Place the meat on the grill with the fat side down and let it cool until the internal temperature reaches 160°F.
5. Remove the meat from the grill and double wrap it with foil. Return it to the grill and cook until the internal temperature reaches 204°F.
6. Remove from grill, unwrap the brisket and let est for 15 minutes.
7. Slice and serve.

Nutritional Information

Calories 270, Total fat 20g, Saturated fat 8g, Total Carbs 3g, Net Carbs 3g, Protein 20g, Sugar 1g, Fiber 0g, Sodium: 1220mg

Grilled Ribeye Steaks

This is a simple and quick recipe that turns out to be very flavorful, juicy and the best steak to serve yourself and your family.
Prep time: 15 minutes, **Cook time:** 35 minutes; **Serves:** 1

Ingredients

➢ 2-inch thick ribeye steaks
➢ Steak rub of choice

Preparation Method

1. Preheat your pellet grill to low smoke.
2. Sprinkle the steak with your favorite steak rub and place it on the grill. Let it smoke for 25 minutes.
3. Remove the steak from the grill and set the temperature to 400°F.
4. Return the steak to the grill and sear it for 5 minutes on each side.
5. Cook until the desired temperature is achieved; 125°F-rare, 145°F-Medium, and 165°F.-Well done.
6. Wrap the steak with foil and let rest for 10 minutes before serving. Enjoy.

Nutritional Information

Calories 225, Total fat 10.4g, Saturated fat 3.6g, Total Carbs 0.2g, Net Carbs 0.2g, Protein 32.5g, Sugar 0g, Fiber 0g, Sodium: 63mg, Potassium 463mg

Grilled Trip tip with java Chophouse

For the lovers of Grilled beef and coffee, this is an amazing recipe for you. The coffee in the seasoning creates a flavourful and crusty bark giving your tri-tip a succulent taste
Prep time: 10 minutes, **Cook time:** 90 minutes; **Serves:** 4

Ingredients

➢ 2 tbsp olive oil
➢ 2 tbsp java chophouse seasoning
➢ 3 lb trip tip roast, fat cap and silver skin removed

Preparation Method

1. Startup your Green Mountain Grill and smoker and set the temperature to 225°F.
2. Rub the roast with olive oil and seasoning then place it on the smoker rack.
3. Smoke until the internal temperature is 140°F.
4. Remove the tri-tip from the smoker and let rest for 10 minutes before serving. Enjoy.

Nutritional Information

Calories 270, Total fat 7g, Saturated fat 2g, Total Carbs 0g, Net Carbs 0g, Protein 23g, Sugar 0g, Fiber 0g, Sodium: 47mg, potassium 289mg

Supper Beef Roast

If you love to be a crowd-pleaser, then this hearty easy recipe is about to make you the hero of the most amazing dinner meal.
Prep time: 5 minutes, **Cook time:** 3 hours; **Serves:** 7

Ingredients

- 3-1/2 beef top round
- 3 tbsp vegetable oil
- Prime rib rub
- 2 cups beef broth
- 1 russet potato, peeled and sliced
- 2 carrots, peeled and sliced
- 2 celery stalks, chopped
- 1 onion, sliced
- 2 thyme sprigs

Preparation Method

1. Rub the roast with vegetable oil and place it on the roasting fat side up. Season with prime rib rub then pour the beef broth.
2. Set the temperature to 500°F and preheat the Green Mountain Grill for 15 minutes with the lid closed.
3. Cook for 30 minutes or until the roast is well seared.
4. Reduce temperature to 225°F. Add the veggies and thyme and cover with foil. Cook for 3 more hours o until the internal temperature reaches 135°F.
5. Remove from the grill and let rest for 10 minutes. Slice against the grain and serve with vegetables and the pan dippings.
6. Enjoy.

Nutritional Information

Calories 697, Total fat 10g, Saturated fat 4.7g, Total Carbs 127g, Net Carbs 3106g, Protein 34g, Sugar 14g, Fiber 22g, Sodium: 3466mg, Potassium 2329mg

Green Mountain Grill Deli-style Roast beef

This is a delish classic roast that easy to make and packed with smoky flavors. You can preserve leftovers in the fridge to make sandwiches all week long.

Prep time: 15 minutes, **Cook time:** 4 hours; **Serves:** 2

Ingredients

- 4lb round-bottomed roast
- 1 tbsp coconut oil
- 1/4 tbsp garlic powder
- 1/4 tbsp onion powder
- 1/4 tbsp thyme
- 1/4 tbsp oregano
- 1/2 tbsp paprika
- 1/2 tbsp salt
- 1/2 tbsp black pepper

Preparation Method

1. Combine all the dry hubs to get a dry rub.
2. Roll the roast in oil then coat with the rub.
3. Set your grill to 185°F and place the roast on the grill.
4. Smoke for 4 hours or until the internal temperature reaches 140°F.
5. Remove the roast from the grill and let rest for 10 minutes.
6. Slice thinly and serve.

Nutritional Information

Calories 90, Total fat 3g, Saturated fat 1g, Total Carbs 0g, Net Carbs 0g, Protein 14g, Sugar 0g, Fiber 0g, Sodium: 420mg

CHAPTER 2

Pork Recipes

Simple Grilled Pork ribs

These are simple but very delicious Grilled pork ribs which surely blow your mind away.
Prep time: 15 minutes, **Cook time:** 5 hours; **Serves:** 7

Ingredients

- ➢ 3 rack baby back ribs
- ➢ 3/4 cup pork and poultry rub
- ➢ 3/4 cup Que BBQ Sauce

Preparation Method

1. Peel the membrane from the backside of the ribs and trim any fat.
2. Season the pork generously with the rub.
3. Set the Green Mountain Grill to 180°F and preheat for 15 minutes with the lid closed.
4. Place the pork ribs on the grill and smoke them for 5 hours.
5. Remove the pork from the grill and wrap them in a foil with the BBQ sauce.
6. Place back the pork and increase the temperature to 350°F. Cook for 45 more minutes.
7. Remove the pork from the grill and let it rest for 20 minutes before serving. Enjoy.

Nutritional Information

Calories 762, Total fat 57g, Saturated fat 17g, Total Carbs 23g, Net Carbs 22.7g, Protein 39g, Sugar 18g, Fiber 0.5g, Sodium: 737mg, Potassium 618mg

Roasted Pork with Balsamic Strawberry Sauce

Are you looking for a romantic dinner for two that you can make in your backyard and with ease? This tender seared pork packed with flavors is a solid choice.
Prep time: 15 minutes, **Cook time:** 35 minutes; **Serves:** 3

Ingredients

- ➢ 2 lb pork tenderloin
- ➢ Salt and pepper to taste

- ➢ 2 tbsp rosemary, dried
- ➢ 2 tbsp olive oil
- ➢ 12 strawberries, fresh
- ➢ 1 cup balsamic vinegar
- ➢ 4 tbsp sugar

Preparation Method

1. Set the Green Mountain Grill to 350°F and preheat for 15 minutes with a closed lid.
2. Meanwhile, rinse the pork and pat it dry. Season with salt, pepper, and rosemary.
3. In an oven skillet, heat oil until smoking. Add the pork and sear on all sides until golden brown.
4. Set the skillet in the grill and cook for 20 minutes or until the meat is no longer pink and the internal temperature is 150°F.
5. Remove the pork from the grill and let rest for 10 minutes.
6. Add berries to the skillet and sear over the stovetop for a minute. Remove the strawberries from the skillet.
7. Add vinegar in the same skillet and scrape any browned bits from the skillet bottom. Bring it to boil then reduce heat to low. Stir in sugar and cook until it has reduced by half.
8. Slice the meat and place the strawberries on top then drizzle vinegar sauce. Enjoy.

Nutritional Information

Calories 244, Total fat 9g, Saturated fat 3g, Total Carbs 15g, Net Carbs 13g, Protein 25g, Sugar 12g, Fiber 2g, Sodium: 159mg

Green Mountain Grill pork crown Roast

This flavorsome meat is the king of all pork roasts. The rub, slow roasting then a spritz of apple juice gives the pork a tangy flavor to perfection.
Prep time: 5 minutes, **Cook time:** 1 hour; **Serves:** 5

Ingredients

- ➢ 13 ribs pork
- ➢ 1/4 cup favorite rub
- ➢ 1 cup apple juice
- ➢ 1 cup Apricot BBQ sauce

Preparation Method

1. Set the wood pellet temperature to 375°F to preheat for 15 minutes with the lid closed.
2. Meanwhile, season the pork with the rub then let sit for 30 minutes.

3. Wrap the tips of each crown roast with foil to prevent the borns from turning black.
4. Place the meat on the grill grate and cook for 90 minutes. Spray apple juice every 30 minutes.
5. When the meat has reached an internal temperature of 125°F remove the foils.
6. Spray the roast with apple juice again and let cook until the internal temperature has reached 135°F.
7. In the last 10 minutes of cooking, baste the roast with BBQ sauce.
8. Remove from the grill and wrap with foil. Let rest for 15 minutes before serving. Enjoy.

Nutritional Information

Calories 240, Total fat 16g, Saturated fat 6g, Total Carbs 0g, Net Carbs 0g, Protein 23g, Sugar 0g, Fiber 0g, Sodium: 50mg

Wet-Rubbed St. Louis Ribs

These spicy pork ribs are easy to make and will win you a blue ribbon in the next family dinner or gathering.
Prep time: 15 minutes, **Cook time:** 4 hours; **Serves:** 3

Ingredients

1/2 cup brown sugar
1 tbsp cumin, ground
1 tbsp Ancho Chile powder
1 tbsp Grilled paprika
1 tbsp garlic salt
3 tbsp balsamic vinegar
1 Rack St. Louis style ribs
2 cup apple juice

Preparation Method

1. Add all the ingredients except ribs in a mixing bowl and mix until well mixed. Place the rub on both sides of the ribs and let sit for 10 minutes.
2. Set the wood pellet temperature to 180°F and preheat for 15 minutes. Smoke the ribs for 2 hours.
3. Increase the temperature to 250°F and wrap the ribs and apple juice with foil or in tinfoil.
4. Place back the pork and cook for an additional 2 hours.
5. Remove from the grill and let rest for 10 minutes before serving. Enjoy.

Calories 210, Total fat 13g, Saturated fat 4g, Total Carbs 0g, Net Carbs 0g, Protein 24g, Sugar 0g, Fiber 0g, Sodium: 85mg

Cocoa Crusted Pork Tenderloin

This wood pellet crusted pork tenderloin is what you need to curb all those pork cravings. It's delicious and easy to prepare.

Prep time: 30 minutes, **Cook time:** 25 minutes; **Serves:** 5

Ingredients

- ➢ 1 pork tenderloin
- ➢ 1/2 tbsp fennel, ground
- ➢ 2 tbsp cocoa powder, unsweetened
- ➢ 1 tbsp Grilled paprika
- ➢ 1/2 tbsp kosher salt
- ➢ 1/2 tbsp black pepper
- ➢ 1 tbsp extra virgin olive oil
- ➢ 3 green onion

Preparation Method

1. Remove the silver skin and the connective tissues from the pork loin.
2. Combine the rest of the ingredients in a mixing bowl, then rub the mixture on the pork. Refrigerate for 30 minutes.
3. Preheat the Green Mountain Grill for 15 minutes with the lid closed.
4. Sear all sides of the loin at the front of the grill then reduce the temperature to 350°F and move the pork to the centre grill.
5. Cook for 15 more minutes or until the internal temperature is 145°F.
6. Remove from grill and let rest for 10 minutes before slicing. Enjoy

Nutritional Information

Calories 264, Total fat 13.1g, Saturated fat 6g, Total Carbs 4.6g, Net Carbs 1.2g, Protein 33g, Sugar 0g, Fiber 3.4g, Sodium: 66mg

Grilled Bacon

Are you a bacon lover? Up your bacon game with this amazing one ingredient quick and simple to make wood pellet bacon

Prep time: 30 minutes, **Cook time:** 25 minutes; **Serves:** 6

Ingredients

➢ 1 lb bacon, thickly cut

Preparation Method

1. Preheat your Green Mountain Grill to 375°F.
2. Line a baking sheet with parchment paper then place the bacon on it in a single layer.
3. Close the lid and bake for 20 minutes. Flip over, close the lid, and bake for an additional 5 minutes.
4. Serve with the favorite side and enjoy.

Nutritional Information

Calories 315, Total fat 14g, Saturated fat 10g, Total Carbs 0g, Net Carbs 0g, Protein 9g, Sugar 0g, Fiber 0g, Sodium: 500mg

Grilled pork Chops

These pork chops are amazingly tender and juicy and are a perfect way to use bone-in chops you will find in your pork.
Prep time: 20 minutes, **Cook time:** 10 minutes; **Serves:** 6

Ingredients

➢ 6 pork chops, thickly cut
➢ BBQ rub

Preparation Method

1. Preheat the wood pellet to 450°F.
2. Season the pork chops generously with the bbq rub. Place the pork chops on the grill and cook for 6 minutes or until the internal temperature reaches 145°F.
3. Remove from the grill and let sit for 10 minutes before serving.
4. Enjoy.

Nutritional Information

Calories 264, Total fat 13g, Saturated fat 6g, Total Carbs 4g, Net Carbs 1g, Protein 33g, Sugar 0g, Fiber 3g, Sodium: 66mg

Wood pellet Blackened Pork Chops

These are delicious blackened pork chops that are cooked on a Green Mountain Grill. They are flavorful, juicy, and above all the simplest.
Prep time: 5 minutes, **Cook time:** 20 minutes; **Serves:** 6

Ingredients

6 pork chops
1/4 cup blackening seasoning
Salt and pepper to taste

Preparation Method

1. Preheat your grill to 375°F.
2. Meanwhile, generously season the pork chops with the blackening seasoning, salt, and pepper.
3. Place the pork chops on the grill and close the lid.
4. Let grill for 8 minutes then flip the chops. Cook until the internal temperature reaches 142°F.
5. Remove the chops from the grill and let rest for 10 minutes before slicing.
6. Serve and enjoy.

Nutritional Information

Calories 333, Total fat 18g, Saturated fat 6g, Total Carbs 1g, Net Carbs 0g, Protein 40g, Sugar 0g, Fiber 1g, Sodium: 3175mg

Teriyaki Pineapple Pork Tenderloin Sliders

These sliders are fantastic for lunch or dinner especially when you grill the pineapple along with the pork.
Prep time: 20 minutes, **Cook time:** 20 minutes; **Serves:** 6

Ingredients

- 1-1/2 lb pork tenderloin
- 1 can pineapple rings
- 1 package king's Hawaiian rolls
- 8 oz teriyaki sauce
- 1-1/2 tbsp salt
- 1 tbsp onion powder
- 1 tbsp paprika
- 1/2 tbsp garlic powder
- 1/2 tbsp cayenne pepper

Preparation Method

1. Add all the ingredients for the rub in a mixing bowl and mix until well mixed. Generously rub the pork loin with the mixture.
2. Heat the pellet to 325°F. Place the meat on a grill and cook while you turn it every 4 minutes.
3. Cook until the internal temperature reaches 145°F.remove from the grill and let it rest for 5 minutes.
4. Meanwhile, open the pineapple can and place the pineapple rings on the grill. Flip the rings when they have a dark brown color.
5. At the same time, half the rolls and place them on the grill and grill them until toasty browned.
6. Assemble the slider by putting the bottom roll first, followed by the pork tenderloin, pineapple ring, a drizzle of sauce, and top with the other roll half.
7. Serve and enjoy.

Nutritional Information

Calories 243, Total fat 5g, Saturated fat 2g, Total Carbs 4g, Net Carbs 15g, Protein 33g, Sugar 10g, Fiber 1g, Sodium: 2447mg

Grilled Tenderloin with fresh herb sauce

This is a really good piece of pork that is liberally seasoned then grilled on a wood pellet giving a juicy and tender meal to serve your family or friends.
Prep time: 10 minutes, **Cook time:** 15 minutes; **Serves:** 4

Ingredients

Pork
➤ 1 pork tenderloin, silver skin removed and dried
➤ BBQ seasoning
Fresh herb sauce
➤ 1 handful basil, fresh
➤ 1/4 tbsp garlic powder
➤ 1/3 cup olive oil
➤ 1/2 tbsp kosher salt

Preparation Method

1. Preheat the Green Mountain Grill to medium heat.
2. Coat the pork with BBQ seasoning then cook on semi-direct heat of the grill. Turn the pork regularly to ensure even cooking.
3. Cook until the internal temperature is 145°F. Remove from the grill and let it rest for 10 minutes.

4. Meanwhile, make the herb sauce by pulsing all the sauce ingredients in a food processor. Pulse for a few times or until well chopped.
5. Slice the pork diagonally and spoon the sauce on top. Serve and enjoy.

Nutritional Information

Calories 300, Total fat 22g, Saturated fat 4g, Total Carbs 13g, Net Carbs 12g, Protein 14g, Sugar 10g, Fiber 1g, Sodium: 791mg

Grilled shredded pork tacos

Are you a taco lover? These grilled tacos may not be easy to make but are worth the time. They are delicious and the best and filling dinner for your family.
Prep time: 15 minutes, **Cook time:** 7 hours; **Serves:** 8

Ingredients

➢ 5 lb pork shoulder, bone-in
Dry Rub
➢ 3 tbsp brown sugar
➢ 1 tbsp salt
➢ 1 tbsp garlic powder
➢ 1 tbsp paprika
➢ 1 tbsp onion powder
➢ 1/4 tbsp cumin
➢ 1 tbsp cayenne pepper

Preparation Method

1. Mix all the dry rub ingredients and rub on the pork shoulder.
2. Preheat the grill to 275°F and cook the pork directly for 6 hours or until the internal temperature has reached 145°F.
3. If you want to fall off the bone tender pork, then cook until the internal temperature is 190°F.
4. Let rest for 10 minutes before serving. Enjoy

Nutritional Information

Calories 566, Total fat 41g, Saturated fat 15g, Total Carbs 4g, Net Carbs 4g, Protein 44g, Sugar 3g, Fiber 0g, Sodium: 659mg

Wood Pellet Togarashi Pork tenderloin

This is an easy pork tenderloin that is grilled in your wood pellet covered in the delicious togarashi seasoning making it a mouthwatering dinner dish.
Prep time: 5 minutes, **Cook time:** 25 minutes; **Serves:** 6

Ingredients

- ➤ 1 Pork tenderloin
- ➤ 1/2tbsp kosher salt
- ➤ 1/4 cup Togarashi seasoning

Preparation Method

1. Cut any excess silver skin from the pork and sprinkle with salt to taste. Rub generously with the togarashi seasoning
2. Place in a preheated oven at 400°F for 25 minutes or until the internal temperature reaches 145°F.
3. Remove from the grill and let rest for 10 minutes before slicing and serving.
4. Enjoy.

Nutritional Information

Calories 390, Total fat 13g, Saturated fat 6g, Total Carbs 4g, Net Carbs 1g, Protein 33g, Sugar 0g, Fiber 3g, Sodium: 66mg

Wood Pellet Pulled Pork

If you are a lover of pulled pork, then this is an ideal choice for you. It's delicious but takes quite some time to cook which is worth it.
Prep time: 15 minutes, **Cook time:** 12 hours; **Serves:** 12

Ingredients

- ➤ 8 lb pork shoulder roast, bone-in
- ➤ BBQ rub
- ➤ 3 cups apple cider, dry hard

Preparation Method

1. Fire up the Green Mountain Grill and set it to smoke.
2. Meanwhile, rub the pork with bbq rub on all sides then place it on the grill grates. cook for 5 hours, flipping it every 1 hour.
3. Increase the heat to 225°F and continue cooking for 3 hours directly on the grate.
4. Transfer the pork to a foil pan and place the apple cider at the bottom of the pan.
5. Cook until the internal temperature reaches 200°F then remove it from the grill. Wrap the pork loosely with foil then let it rest for 1 hour.
6. Remove the fat layer and use forks to shred it.
7. Serve and enjoy.

Nutritional Information

Calories 912, Total fat 65g, Saturated fat 24g, Total Carbs 7g, Net Carbs 7g, Protein 70g, Sugar 6g, Fiber 0g, Sodium: 208mg

Grilled Pork Ribs

Honestly, this is my number one pork recipe. It's easy plus the Grilled ribs are just amazing.
Prep time: 15minutes, **Cook time:** 10 hours; **Serves:** 4

Ingredients

- 2 racks baby back ribs
- 1 cup homemade BBQ rub
- 24 oz hard apple cider
- 1 cup dark brown sugar
- 2 batches homemade BBQ sauce

Preparation Method

1. Set your wood pellet to smoke.
2. Remove the membrane from the pork ribs then generously coat with bbq sauce.
3. Smoke at 175°F for 5 hours. Increase the grill temperature to 225°F.
4. Transfer the pork to a high sided pan that has been sprayed with cooking spray.
5. Pour over the apple cider and rub the pork with sugar. Cover the pan with foil and place it back to the grill. Cook for 4 more hours.
6. Transfer the ribs from the pan to the grill grate and increase the temperature to 300°F.
7. Brush the ribs with BBQ sauce 3 times in the next 1 hour. Remove the ribs from the grill and serve them. Enjoy.

Nutritional Information

Calories 1073, Total fat 42g, Saturated fat 15g, Total Carbs 111g, Net Carbs 108g, Protein 61g, Sugar 99g, Fiber 3g, Sodium: 1663mg

Grilled Spicy Candied Bacon

This is the simplest and quickest crowd-pleaser snack recipe you will ever find. Serve them when your house is full of movies or football fans.
Prep time: 5 minutes, **Cook time:** 35 minutes; **Serves:** 6

Ingredients

- ➤ 1 lb centre cut bacon
- ➤ 1/2 cup dark brown sugar
- ➤ 1/2 cup maple syrup
- ➤ 1 tbsp sriracha hot sauce
- ➤ 1/2 tbsp cayenne pepper

Preparation Method

1. In a mixing bowl, combine sugar, maple syrup, sriracha sauce, and cayenne pepper.
2. Preheat the Green Mountain Grill to 300°F.
3. Line a baking pan with parchment paper and lay the bacon on it in a single layer. Brush the bacon with the sugar mixture until well coated.
4. Place the baking pan in the grill and cook for 20 minutes. Flip the bacon and cook for 15 more minutes.
5. Remove the bacon from the grill and let cool for 10 minutes before removing from the baking pan and serving.
6. Enjoy.

Nutritional Information

Calories 458, Total fat 14g, Saturated fat 10g, Total Carbs 37g, Net Carbs 37g, Protein 9g, Sugar 33g, Fiber 0g, Sodium: 565mg

CHAPTER 3

Grilled Lamb chops

These are absolutely delicious and the most flavorful lamb chops which are first Grilled then grilled. You can cut into individual appetizer lollipops or serve two pieces for an entree.

Prep time: 10 minutes, **Cook time:** 50 minutes; **Serves:** 4

Ingredients

- 1 rack of lamb, fat trimmed
- 2 tbsp rosemary, fresh
- 2 tbsp sage, fresh
- 1 tbsp garlic cloves, roughly chopped
- 1/2 tbsp salt
- 1/2 tbsp pepper, coarsely ground
- 1/4 cup olive oil
- 1 tbsp honey

Preparation Method

1. Preheat your wood pellet smoker to 225°F using a fruitwood.
2. Combine all the ingredients except the lamb in a food processor. Liberally apply the mixture on the lamb.
3. Place the lamb on the smoker for 45 minutes or until the internal temperature reaches 120°F.
4. Sear the lamb on the grill for 2 minutes per side. let rest for 5 minutes before serving.
5. Slice and enjoy.

Nutritional Information

Calories 704, Total fat 56g, Saturated fat 14g, Total Carbs 24g, Net Carbs 23g, Protein 27g, Sugar 6g, Fiber 1g, Sodium: 124mg

Grilled Lamb Shoulder

Are you a lamb lover? If yes this lamb shoulder will brow away your mind. It's delicious with a traditional smoke flavor that will make you want to cook it more.

Prep time: 10 minutes, **Cook time:** 1hour 30 minutes; **Serves:** 7

Ingredients

For Grilled Lamb Shoulder
- 5 lb lamb shoulder, boneless and excess fat trimmed
- 2 tbsp kosher salt
- 2 tbsp black pepper
- 1 tbsp rosemary, dried

The Injection
- 1 cup apple cider vinegar

The Spritz
- 1 cup apple cider vinegar
- 1 cup apple juice

Preparation Method

1. Preheat the wood pellet smoker with a water pan to 225° F.
2. Rinse the lamb in cold water then pat it dry with a paper towel. Inject vinegar to the lamb.
3. Pat the lamb dry again and rub with oil, salt black pepper and rosemary. Tie with kitchen twine.
4. Smoke uncovered for 1 hour then spritz after every 15 minutes until the internal temperature reaches 195° F.
5. Remove the lamb from the grill and place it on a platter. Let cool before shredding it and enjoying it with your favorite side.

Nutritional Information

Calories 243, Total fat 19g, Saturated fat 8g, Total Carbs 0g, Net Carbs 0g, Protein 17g, Sugar 0g, Fiber 1g, Sodium: 63mg, Potassium 234mg

Grilled Pulled Lamb Sliders

The lamb shoulder is Grilled to perfection then pulled to make incredibly Grilled and pulled lamb sliders.
Prep time: 10 minutes, **Cook time:** 7 hour**s; Serves:** 7

Ingredients

For the Lamb's shoulder
- 5 lb lamb shoulder, boneless
- 1/2 cup olive oil
- 1/4 cup dry rub
- 10 oz spritz

The Dry Rub
- 1/3 cup kosher salt
- 1/3 cup pepper, ground

- ➤ 1-1/3 cup garlic, granulated

The Spritz
- ➤ 4 oz Worcestershire sauce
- ➤ 6 oz apple cider vinegar

Preparation Method

1. Preheat the wood pellet smoker with a water bath to 250° F.
2. Trim any fat from the lamb then rub with oil and dry rub.
3. Place the lamb on the smoker for 90 minutes then spritz with a spray bottle every 30 minutes until the internal temperature reaches 165° F.
4. Transfer the lamb shoulder to a foil pan with the remaining spritz liquid and cover tightly with foil.
5. Place back in the smoker and smoke until the internal temperature reaches 200° F.
6. Remove from the smoker and let rest for 30 minutes before pulling the lamb and serving with slaw, bun, or aioli. Enjoy

Nutritional Information

Calories 339, Total Fat 22, Saturated fat 7g, Total Carbs 16g, Net Carbs 15g, Protein 18g, Sugar 2g, Fiber 1g, Sodium: 459mg

Grilled Lamb Meatballs

These flavorful, moist Grilled lamb meatballs offer a brilliant way to jazz up any pasta dish or pita sandwich
Prep time: 10 minutes, **Cook time:** 1 hour; **Serves:** 5

Ingredients

- ➤ 1 lb lamb shoulder, ground
- ➤ 3 garlic cloves, finely diced
- ➤ 3 tbsp shallot, diced
- ➤ 1 tbsp salt
- ➤ 1 egg
- ➤ 1/2 tbsp pepper
- ➤ 1/2 tbsp cumin
- ➤ 1/2 tbsp Grilled paprika
- ➤ 1/4 tbsp red pepper flakes
- ➤ 1/4 tbsp cinnamon, ground
- ➤ 1/4 cup panko breadcrumbs

Preparation Method

1. Set the wood pellet smoker to 250° F using a fruitwood.
2. In a mixing bowl, combine all meatball ingredients until well mixed.

3. Form small-sized balls and place them on a baking sheet. Place the baking sheet in the smoker and smoke until the internal temperature reaches 160°F.
4. Remove from the smoker and serve. Enjoy.

Nutritional Information

Calories 73, Total fat 5.2g, Saturated fat 1.6g, Total Carbs 1.5g, Net Carbs 1.4g, Protein 4.9g, Sugar 0g, Fiber 0.1g, Sodium: 149mg, Potassium 72mg

Crown rack of lamb

The presentation of this crown rack lamb is incredible and takes your grilling to the next level. What more, cooking this lamb with a wood pellet guarantees great results.
Prep time: 10 minutes, **Cook time:** 30 minutes; **Serves:** 6

Ingredients

- 2 racks of lamb, frenched
- 1 tbsp garlic, crushed
- 1 tbsp rosemary, finely chopped
- 1/4 cup olive oil
- 2 feet twine

Preparation Method

1. Rinse the racks with cold water then pat them dry with a paper towel.
2. Lay the racks on a flat board then score between each bone, about ¼ inch down.
3. In a mixing bowl, mix garlic, rosemary, and oil then generously brush on the lamb.
4. Take each lamb rack and bend it into a semicircle forming a crown-like shape.
5. Use the twine to wrap the racks about 4 times starting from the base to the top. Make sure you tie the twine tightly to keep the racks together.
6. Preheat the wood pellet to 400-450°F then place the lamb racks on a baking dish. Plac ethe baing dish on the pellet grill.
7. Cook for 10 minutes then reduce temperature to 300°F. cook for 20 more minutes or until the internal temperature reaches 130°F.
8. Remove the lamb rack from the wood pellet and let rest for 15 minutes.
9. Serve when hot with veggies and potatoes. Enjoy.

Nutritional Information

Calories 390, Total fat 35g, Saturated fat 15g, Total Carbs 0g, Net Carbs 0g, Protein 17g, Sugar 0g, Fiber 0g, Sodium: 65mg

Grilled Leg of Lamb

Smoking a whole amb leg could not be any easier than in this recipe. The leg comes out delicious packed with a smoke flavor that will leave everyone asking for more.
Prep time: 15 minutes, **Cook time:** 3hourss; **Serves:** 6

Ingredients

- 1 leg lamb, boneless
- 4 garlic cloves, minced
- 2 tbsp salt
- 1 tbsp black pepper, freshly ground
- 2 tbsp oregano
- 1 tbsp thyme
- 2 tbsp olive oil

Preparation Method

1. Trim any excess fat from the lamb and tie the lamb using twine to form a nice roast.
2. In a mixing bowl, mix garlic, spices, and oil. Rub all over the lamb, wrap with a plastic bag then refrigerate for an hour to marinate.
3. Place the lamb on a smoker set at 250° F. smoke the lamb for 4 hours or until the internal temperature reaches 145° F.
4. Remove from the smoker and let rest to cool. Serve and enjoy.

Nutritional Information

Calories 356, Total fat16 g, Saturated fat 5g, Total Carbs 3g, Net Carbs 2g, Protein 49g, Sugar 1g, Fiber 1g, Sodium: 2474mg

Grilled Aussie Leg of Lamb Roast

Did you that grilling a leg of lamb is as easy as roasting it in the oven? The end results though are outstanding. The smoke flavor makes the lamb irresistibly addictive
Prep time: 30 minutes, **Cook time:** 2 hours; **Serves:** 8

Ingredients

- 5 lb Aussie leg of lamb, boneless

Grilled Paprika Rub
- 1 tbsp raw sugar
- 1 tbsp kosher salt
- 1 tbsp black pepper
- 1 tbsp Grilled paprika
- 1 tbsp garlic powder

- ➤ 1 tbsp rosemary, dried
- ➤ 1 tbsp onion powder
- ➤ 1tbsp cumin
- ➤ 1/2 tbsp cayenne pepper

Roasted Carrots

- ➤ 1 bunch rainbow carrots
- ➤ Olive oil
- ➤ Salt
- ➤ pepper

Preparation Method

1. Heat the Green Mountain Grill to 375° F.
2. Trim any excess fat from the lamb.
3. Combine all the rub ingredients and rub all over the lamb. Place the lamb on the grill and smoke for 2 hours.
4. Toss the carrots in oil, salt, and pepper then add to the grill after the lamb has cooked for 1 ½ hour.
5. Cook until the roast internal temperature reaches 135° F. Remove the lamb from the grill and cover with foil. Let rest for 30 minutes.
6. Remove the carrots from the grill once soft and serve with the lamb. Enjoy.

Nutritional Information

Calories 257, Total fat 8g, Saturated fat 2g, Total Carbs 6g, Net Carbs 5g, Protein 37g, Sugar 3g, Fiber 1g, Sodium: 431mg, Potassium 666mg

Simple Grilled Lamb Chops

These simple and tasty simple grilled lamb chops are all you need for your family dinner. Making it under the moonlight on your Green Mountain Grill makes it more fun.
Prep time: 10 minutes, **Cook time:** 6 minutes; **Serves:** 6

Ingredients

- ➤ 1/4 cup distilled white vinegar
- ➤ 2 tbsp salt
- ➤ 1/2 tbsp black pepper
- ➤ 1 tbsp garlic, minced
- ➤ 1 onion, thinly sliced
- ➤ 2 tbsp olive oil
- ➤ 2lb lamb chops

Preparation Method

1. In a resealable bag, mix vinegar, salt, black pepper, garlic, sliced onion, and oil until all salt has dissolved.
2. Add the lamb chops and toss until well coated. Place in the fridge to marinate for 2 hours.
3. Preheat the Green Mountain Grill to high heat.
4. Remove the lamb from the fridge and discard the marinade. Wrap any exposed bones with foil.
5. Grill the lamb for 3 minutes per side. You can also broil in a broiler for more crispness.
6. Serve and enjoy

Nutritional Information

Calories 519, Total fat 44.8g, Saturated fat 18g, Total Carbs 2.3g, Net Carbs 1.9g, Protein 25g, Sugar1g, Fiber 0.4g, Sodium: 861mg, Potassium 359mg

Grilled Lamb with Brown Sugar Glaze

A sweet and savory lamb meal that is perfect for a spring meal with vegetables and noodles. Make sure to marinate the chops for an hour for the awesome end result.
Prep time: 15 minutes, **Cook time:** 10 minutes; **Serves:** 4

Ingredients

- 1/4 cup brown sugar
- 2 tbsp ginger, ground
- 2 tbsp tarragon, dried
- 1 tbs cinnamon, ground
- 1 tbsp black pepper, ground
- 1 tbsp garlic powder
- 1/2 tbsp salt
- 4 lamb chops

Preparation Method

1. In a mixing bowl, mix sugar, ginger, dried tarragon, cinnamon, black pepper, garlic, and salt.
2. Rub the lamb chops with the seasoning and place it on a plate.refrigerate for an hour to marinate.
3. Preheat the grill to high heat then brush the grill grate with oil.
4. Arrange the lamb chops on the grill grate in a single layer and cook for 5 minutes on each side.
5. Serve and enjoy.

Calories 241, Total fat 13.1g, Saturated fat 6g, Total Carbs 15.8g, Net Carbs 15.1g, Protein 14.6g, Sugar 14g, Fiber 0.7g, Sodium: 339mg, Potassium 257mg

Grilled leg of lambs Steaks

These delicious and very tender lamb steaks are a real crowd-pleaser. Make this dinner meal for your family or friends coming over.
Prep time: 10 minutes, **Cook time:** 10 minutes; **Serves:** 4

Ingredients

- 4 lamb steaks, bone-in
- 1/4 cup olive oil
- 4 garlic cloves, minced
- 1 tbsp rosemary, freshly chopped
- Salt and black pepper

Preparation Method

1. Place the lamb in a shallow dish in a single layer. Top with oil, garlic cloves, rosemary, salt, and black pepper then flip the steaks to cover on both sides.
2. Let sit for 30 minutes to marinate.
3. Preheat the Green Mountain Grill to high and brush the grill grate with oil.
4. Place the lamb steaks on the grill grate and cook until browned and the internal is slightly pink. The internal temperature should be 140°F.
5. Let rest for 5 minutes before serving. Enjoy.

Nutritional Information

Calories 327, Total Fat 21.9g, Saturated fat 5g, Total Carbs 1.7g, Net Carbs 1.5g, Protein 29.6g, Sugar 0g, Fiber 0.2g, Sodium: 112mg, Potassium 410mg

Grilled Lamb Loin Chops

Don't let the small size of these lamb chops foo you. They are packed with flavor and are simply the best to serve in a family or friends gathering alongside veggies and another side.
Prep time: 10 minutes, **Cook time:** 10 minutes; **Serves:** 6

Ingredients

- 2 tbsp herbs de Provence

- ➢ 1-1/2 tbsp olive oil
- ➢ 2 garlic cloves, minced
- ➢ 2 tbsp lemon juice
- ➢ 5 oz lamb loin chops
- ➢ Salt and black pepper to taste

Preparation Method

1. In a small mixing bowl, mix herbs de Provence, oil, garlic, and juice. Rub the mixture on the lamb chops then refrigerate for an hour.
2. Preheat the Green Mountain Grill to medium-high then lightly oil the grill grate.
3. Season the lamb chops with salt and black pepper.
4. Place the lamb chops on the grill and cook for 4 minutes on each side.
5. Remove the chops from the grill and place them in an aluminum covered plate. Let rest for 5 minutes before serving. Enjoy.

Nutritional Information

Calories 579, Total fat 43.9g, Saturated fat 17g, Total Carbs 0.7g, Net Carbs 0.7g, Protein 42.5g, Sugar 0g, Fiber 0g, Sodium: 169mg, Potassium 560mg

Spicy Chinese Cumin Lamb Skewers

This is a Chinese traditional lamb skewer that is a street fair jus like kebabs which are cooked all over the world. Enjoy these lamb skewers with a bottle of beer to kick off the evening in a great way.

Prep time: 20 minutes, **Cook time:** 6 minutes; **Serves:** 10

Ingredients

- ➢ 1lb lamb shoulder, cut into ½ inch pieces
- ➢ 10 skewers
- ➢ 2 tbsp ground cumin
- ➢ 2 tbsp red pepper flakes
- ➢ 1 tbsp salt

Preparation Method

1. Thread the lamb pieces onto skewers.
2. Preheat the Green Mountain Grill to medium heat and lightly oil the grill grate.
3. Place the skewers on the grill grate and cook while turning occasionally. Sprinkle cumin, pepper flakes, and salt every time you turn the skewer.
4. Cook for 6 minutes or until nicely browned.
5. Serve and enjoy.

Green Mountain Grill Dale's Lamb

This dales lamb is not only easy to make but also wonderfully flavourful. The dish has a gourmet flavor that will please people who don't like the taste of lamb.
Prep time: 15 minutes, **Cook time:** 50 minutes; **Serves:** 8

Ingredients

- 2/3 cup lemon juice
- 1/2 cup brown sugar
- 1/4 cup Dijon mustard
- 1/4 cup soy sauce
- 1/4 cup olive oil
- 2 garlic cloves, minced
- 1 piece ginger root, freshly sliced
- 1 tbsp salt
- 1/2 tbsp black pepper, ground
- 5 lb leg of lamb, butterflied

Preparation Method

1. In a mixing bowl, mix lemon juice, sugar, dijon mustard, sauce, oil, garlic cloves, ginger root, salt, and pepper.
2. Place the lamb in a dish and pour the seasoning mixture over it. Cover the dish and put in a fridge to marinate for 8 hours.
3. Preheat a Green Mountain Grill to medium heat. Drain the marinade from the dish and bring it to boil in a small saucepan.
4. Reduce heat and let simmer while whisking occasionally.
5. Oil the grill grate and place the lamb on it. Cook for 50 minutes or until the internal temperature reaches 145° F while turning occasionally.
6. Slice the lamb and cover with the marinade. Serve and enjoy.

Nutritional Information

Calories 451, Total fat 27.2g, Saturated fat 9.5g, Total Carbs 17.8g, Net Carbs 17.6g, Protein 32.4g, Sugar 14g, Fiber 0.2g, Sodium: 1015mg, Potassium 455mg

Garlic and Rosemary Grilled Lamb Chops

Thes e grilled lamb chops are really delicious and cooked perfectly. If you want to surprise your spouse or family with an elegant dinner, this is the best choice
Prep time: 10 minutes, **Cook time:** 20 minutes; **Serves:** 4

Ingredients

- 2 lb lamb loin, thick-cut
- 4 garlic cloves, minced
- 1 tbsp kosher salt
- 1/2 tbsp black pepper
- 1 lemon zest
- 1/4 cup olive oil

Preparation Method

1. In a small mixing bowl, mix garlic, lemon zest, oil, salt, and black pepper then pour the mixture over the lamb.
2. Flip the lamb chops to make sure they are evenly coated. Place the chops in the fridge to marinate for an hour.
3. Preheat the Green Mountain Grill to high heat then sear the lamb for 3 minutes on each side.
4. Reduce the heat and cook the chops for 6 minutes or until the internal temperature reaches 150° F.
5. Remove the lamb from the grill and wrap it in a foil. Let it rest for 5 minutes before serving. Enjoy.

Nutritional Information

Calories 171.5, Total fat 7.8g, Saturated fat 2.5g, Total Carbs 0.4g, Net Carbs 0.3g, Protein 23.2g, Sugar 0g, Fiber 0.1g, Sodium: 72.8mg, Potassium 393.8mg

Grilled LambChops

These lamb chops are grilled with rosemary and thyme marinade giving it a fantastic flavourful dinner meal.
Prep time: 1 hour, **Cook time:** 8 minutes; **Serves:** 3

Ingredients

- 2 garlic cloves, crushed
- 1 tbsp rosemary leaves, fresh chopped
- 2 tbsp olive oil
- 1 tbsp lemon juice, fresh
- 1 tbsp thyme leaves, fresh

- ➤ 1 tbsp salt
- ➤ 9 lamb loin chops

Preparation Method

1. Add the garlic, rosemary, oil, juice, salt, and thyme in a food processor. Pulse until smooth.
2. Rub the marinade on the lamb chops both sides and let marinate for 1 hour in a fridge. Remove from the fridge and let sit at room temperature for 20 minutes before cooking.
3. Preheat your wood pellet smoker to high heat. smoke the lamb chops for 5 minutes on each side.
4. Sear the lamb chops for 3 minutes on each side. Remove from the grill and serve with a green salad.

Nutritional Information

Calories 1140, Total fat 99g, Saturated fat 41g, Total Carbs 1g, Net Carbs 1g, Protein 55g, Sugar0g, Fiber 0g, Sodium: 965mg, Potassium 739mg

CHAPTER 4

Poultry Recipes

Grilled Chicken Kabobs

These Grilled chicken kabobs are super easy to make, juicy, and above all tender. The good news is the marinade is made with fresh ingredients from your pantry.
Prep time: 45 minutes, **Cook time:** 12 minutes**; Serves:** 6

Ingredients

- 1/2 cup olive oil
- 2 tbsp white vinegar
- 1 tbsp lemon juice
- 1-1/2 tbsp salt
- 1/2 tbsp pepper, coarsely ground
- 2 tbsp chives, freshly chopped
- 1-1/2 tbsp thyme, freshly chopped
- 2 tbsp Italian parsley freshly chopped
- 1tbsp garlic, minced

Kabobs

- 1 each orange, red, and yellow pepper
- 1-1/2 lb chicken breast, boneless and skinless
- 12 crimini mushrooms

Preparation Method

1. In a mixing bowl, add all the marinade ingredients and mix well. Toss the chicken and mushrooms in the marinade then refrigerate for 30 minutes.
2. Meanwhile, soak the skewers in hot water. Remove the chicken from the fridge and start assembling the kabobs.
3. Preheat your wood pellet to 450°F.
4. Grill the kabobs in the wood pellet for 6 minutes, flip them and grill for 6 more minutes.
5. Remove from the grill and let rest. Heat up the naan bread on the grill for 2 minutes.
6. Serve and enjoy.

Nutritional Information

Calories 165, Total fat 13g, Saturated fat 2g, Total Carbs 1g, Net Carbs 1g, Protein 33g, Sugar 0g, Fiber 0g, Sodium: 582mg

Grilled Chicken

If you are a grilled chicken lover, this is going to be the best grilled and roasted chicken you have ever had.
Prep time: 10 minutes, **Cook time:** 1 hour 10 minutes; **Serves:** 6

Ingredients

- 5 lb whole chicken
- 1/2 cup oil
- Chicken rub

Preparation Method

1. Preheat your wood pellet on smoke with the lid open for 5 minutes. Close the lid, increase the temperature to 450°F and preheat for 15 more minutes.
2. Tie the chicken legs together with the baker's twine then rub the chicken with oil and coat with chicken rub.
3. Place the chicken on the grill with the breast side up.
4. Grill the chicken for 70 minutes without opening it or until the internal temperature reaches 165°F.
5. Remove the chicken from the grill and let it rest for 15 minutes before serving.
6. Enjoy.

Nutritional Information

Calories 935, Total fat 53g, Saturated fat 15g, Total Carbs 0g, Net Carbs 0g, Protein 107g, Sugar 0g, Fiber 0g, Sodium: 320mg

Wood pellet chicken breasts

These easy, quick to prepare and delicious chicken breasts are all you need to serve your family for lunch or dinner.
Prep time: 10 minutes, **Cook time:** 15 minutes; **Serves:** 6

Ingredients

- 3 chicken breasts
- 1 tbsp avocado oil
- 1/4 tbsp garlic powder
- 1/4 tbsp onion powder
- 3/4 tbsp salt
- 1/4 tbsp pepper

Preparation Method

1. Preheat your pellet to 375°F.

2. Half the chicken breasts lengthwise then coat with avocado oil.
3. Season with onion powder, garlic powder, salt, and pepper on all sides.
4. Place the chicken on the grill and cook for 7 minutes on each side or until the internal temperature reaches 165°F.
5. Serve and enjoy.

Nutritional Information

Calories 120, Total fat 4g, Saturated fat 1g, Total Carbs 0g, Net Carbs 0g, Protein 19g, Sugar 0g, Fiber 0g, Sodium: 309mg

Grilled Spatchcock Turkey

Trust me this delicious, tender, moist, and evenly cooked spatchcock turkey will be the meal of the day during your Thanksgiving gathering.
Prep time: 30 minutes, **Cook time:** 1 hour 45 minutes; **Serves:** 6

Ingredients

➢ 1 whole turkey
➢ 1/2 cup oil
➢ 1/4 cup chicken rub
➢ 1 tbsp onion powder
➢ 1 tbsp garlic powder
➢ 1 tbsp rubbed sage

Preparation Method

1. Preheat your Green Mountain Grill to high.
2. Meanwhile, place the turkey on a platter with the breast side down then cut on either side of the backbone to remove the spine.
3. Flip the turkey and season on both sides then place it on the preheated grill or on a pan if you want to catch the drippings.
4. Grill on high for 30 minutes, reduce the temperature to 325°F, and grill for 45 more minutes or until the internal temperature reaches 165°F
5. Remove from the grill and let rest for 20 minutes before slicing and serving. Enjoy.

Nutritional Information

Calories 156, Total fat 16g, Saturated fat 2g, Total Carbs 1g, Net Carbs 1g, Protein 2g, Sugar 0g, Fiber 0g, Sodium: 19mg

Grilled Cornish Hens

These easy to prepare cornish hens are awesomely perfect to split between two people or to preserve one for later. Use your favorite rub for an enjoyable dinner meal.
Prep time: 10 minutes, **Cook time:** 1 hour; **Serves:** 6

Ingredients

- ➤ 6 cornish hens
- ➤ 3 tbsp avocado oil
- ➤ 6 tbsp rub of choice

Preparation Method

1. Fire up the wood pellet and preheat it to 275°F.
2. Rub the hens with oil then coat generously with rub. Place the hens on the grill with the chest breast side down.
3. Smoke for 30 minutes. Flip the hens and increase the grill temperature to 400°F. Cook until the internal temperature reaches 165°F.
4. Remove from the grill and let rest for 10 minutes before serving. Enjoy.

Nutritional Information

Calories 696, Total fat 50g, Saturated fat 13g, Total Carbs 1g, Net Carbs 1g, Protein 57g, Sugar 0g, Fiber 0g, Sodium: 165mg

Grilled and fried chicken wings

These chicken wings will leave you leaking your fingers clean. They are super crispy, tender, juicy and the smoke flavor is a golden ticket.
Prep time: 10 minutes, **Cook time:** 2 hours; **Serves:** 6

Ingredients

- ➤ 3 lb chicken wings
- ➤ 1 tbsp goya adobo all-purpose seasoning
- ➤ Sauce of your choice

Preparation Method

1. Fire up your Green Mountain Grill and set it to smoke.
2. Meanwhile, coat the chicken wings with adobo all-purpose seasoning. Place the chicken on the grill and smoke for 2 hours ensuring you turn halfway through the smoke.
3. Remove the wings from the grill.

4. Preheat oil to 375°F in a frying pan. Drop the wings in batches and let fry for 5 minutes or until the skin is crispy.
5. Remove from oil and let drain before serving with your favorite sauce. Enjoy.

Nutritional Information

Calories 755, Total fat 55g, Saturated fat 20g, Total Carbs 24g, Net Carbs 23g, Protein 39g, Sugar 2g, Fiber 1g, Sodium: 1747mg

Grilled Buffalo Chicken Leg

These delicious chicken legs are the most economical way of enjoying buffalo wings without compromising the sweet flavors
Prep time: 5 minutes, **Cook time:** 25 minutes; **Serves:** 6

Ingredients

➢ 12 chicken legs
➢ 1/2 tbsp salt
➢ 1 tbsp buffalo seasoning
➢ 1 cup buffalo sauce

Preparation Method

1. Preheat your Green Mountain Grill to 325°F.
2. Toss the legs in salt and buffalo seasoning then place them on the preheated grill.
3. Grill for 40 minutes ensuring you turn them twice through the cooking.
4. Brush the legs with buffalo sauce and cook for an additional 10 minutes or until the internal temperature reaches 165°F.
5. Remove the legs from the grill, brush with more sauce, and serve when hot. Enjoy with ranch, celery or blue cheese.

Nutritional Information

Calories 956, Total fat 47g, Saturated fat 13g, Total Carbs 1g, Net Carbs 1g, Protein 124g, Sugar 0g, Fiber 0g, Sodium: 1750mg

Wood Pellet Chile Lime Chicken

I just might have a great idea for your dinner tonight, the wood pellet chile lime chicken. Its easy, moist, and very flavorful.
Prep time: 2 minutes, **Cook time:** 15 minutes; **Serves:** 1

Ingredients

- 1 chicken breast
- 1 tbsp oil
- 1 tbsp chile-lime seasoning

Preparation Method

1. Preheat your wood pellet to 400°F.
2. Brush the chicken breast with oil on all sides.
3. Sprinkle with seasoning and salt to taste.
4. Grill for 7 minutes per side or until the internal temperature reaches 165°F.
5. Serve when hot or cold and enjoy.

Nutritional Information

Calories 131, Total fat 5g, Saturated fat 1g, Total carbs 4g, Net carbs 3g, Protein 19g, Sugar 1g, Fiber 1g, Sodium: 235mg

Wood pellet Sheet pan Chicken Fajitas

Cooking delicious food for a large crowd is always a big challenge but do not have to worry anymore. This sheet pan fajita is the way to go.
Prep time: 10 minutes, **Cook time:** 10 minutes; **Serves:** 10

Ingredients

- 2 tbsp oil
- 2 tbsp chile margarita seasoning
- 1 tbsp salt
- 1/2 tbsp onion powder
- 1/2 tbsp garlic, granulated
- 2 lb chicken breast, thinly sliced
- 1 red bell pepper, seeded and sliced
- 1 orange bell pepper
- 1 onion, sliced

Preparation Method

1. Preheat the wood pellet to 450°F.
2. Meanwhile, mix oil and seasoning then toss the chicken and the peppers.
3. Line a sheet pan with foil then place it in the preheated grill. Let it heat for 10 minutes with the grill's lid closed.
4. Open the grill and place the chicken with the veggies on the pan in a single layer.
5. Cook for 10 minutes or until the chicken is cooked and no longer pink.
6. Remove from grill and serve with tortilla or your favorite fixings.

Nutritional Information

Calories 211, Total fat 6g, Saturated fat 1g, Total carbs 5g, Net carbs 4g, Protein29g, Sugar 4g, Fiber 1g, Sodium: 360mg

Buffalo Chicken Flatbread

The tender chunks of chicken, a sauce that gives a nice kick, and a lot of cheese covering the bread give you a golden ticket for a succulent dinner.
Prep time: 5 minutes, **Cook time:** 30 minutes; **Serves:** 6

Ingredients

- 6 mini pita bread
- 1-1/2 cups buffalo sauce
- 4 cups chicken breasts, cooked and cubed
- 3 cups mozzarella cheese
- Blue cheese for drizzling

Preparation Method

1. Preheat the Green Mountain Grill to 375-400°F.
2. Place the breads on a flat surface and evenly spread sauce over all of them.
3. In a mixing bowl, toss the chicken with the remaining buffalo sauce and place them on the pita breads.
4. Top with cheese then place the breads on the grill but indirectly from the heat. Closs the grill lid.
5. Cook for 7 minutes or until the cheese has melted and the edges are toasty.
6. Remove from grill and drizzle with blue cheese. Serve and enjoy.

Nutritional Information

Calories 254, Total fat 13g, Saturated fat 6g, Total carbs 4g, Net carbs 1g, Protein 33g, Sugar 0g, Fiber 3g, Sodium: 66mg

Grilled Buffalo Chicken

This is good news for buffalo chicken wings lovers. These wings are tender, juicy, and easy to make with homemade Cholula buffalo sauce
Prep time: 5 minutes, **Cook time:** 20 minutes; **Serves:** 6

Ingredients

- 5 chicken breasts, boneless and skinless
- 2 tbsp homemade bbq rub
- 1 cup homemade Cholula buffalo sauce

Preparation Method

1. Preheat the Green Mountain Grill to 400°F.
2. Slice the chicken into long strips and season with bbq rub.
3. Place the chicken on the grill and paint both sides with buffalo sauce.
4. Cook for 4 minutes with the grill closed. Cook while flipping and painting with buffalo sauce every 5 minutes until the internal temperature reaches 165°F.
5. Remove from the grill and serve when warm. Enjoy.

Nutritional Information

Calories 176, Total fat 4g, Saturated fat 1g, Total carbs 1g, Net carbs 1g, Protein 32g, Sugar 1g, Fiber 0g, Sodium: 631mg

Beer Can Chicken

This is a flavourful, super moist whole grilled chicken that you and your family or friends will love.
Prep time: 10 minutes, **Cook time:** 1 hour 15 minutes; **Serves:** 6

Ingredients

- 5 lb chicken
- 1/2 cup dry chicken rub
- 1 can beer

Preparation Method

1. Preheat your Green Mountain Grill on smoke for 5 minutes with the lid open. Close the lid and preheat the grill until the temperature reaches 450°F.
2. Pour out half of the beer then shove the can in the chicken and use the legs like a tripod.
3. Place the chicken on the grill and grill until the internal temperature reaches 165°F.
4. Remove from the grill and let rest for 20 minutes before serving. Enjoy.

Nutritional Information

Calories 882, Total fat 51g, Saturated fat 14g, Total carbs 2g, Net carbs 2g, Protein 94g, Sugar 0g, Fiber 0g, Sodium: 279mg

Wood pellet Chicken wings with spicy Miso

These chicken wings smothered in the marinade then grilled will leave your taste buds jumping in joy and your family asking for more.
Prep time: 15 minutes, **Cook time:** 25 minutes; **Serves:** 6

Ingredients

- 2 lb chicken wings
- 3/4 cup soy
- 1/2 cup pineapple juice
- 1 tbsp sriracha
- 1/8 cup miso
- 1/8 cup gochujang
- 1/2 cup water
- 1/2 cup oil
- togarashi

Preparation Method

1. In a mixing bowl, mix all ingredients then toss the chicken wings until they are well coated.refrigerate for 12 minutes.
2. Preheat your Green Mountain Grill to 375°F.
3. Place the chicken wings on the grill grates and close the lid. Cook until the internal temperature reaches 165°F.
4. Remove the wings from the grill and sprinkle with togarashi.
5. Serve when hot and enjoy.

Nutritional Information

Calories 704, Total fat 56g, Saturated fat 14g, Total carbs 24g, Net carbs 23g, Protein 27g, Sugar 6g, Fiber 1g, Sodium: 124mg

Barbecue Chicken wings

I prefer my chicken wings grilled instead of being deep-fried. The wings get crispy on the outside with a moist, flavorful, and tender inside.
Prep time: 10 minutes, **Cook time:** 15 minutes; **Serves:** 4

Ingredients

- Fresh chicken wings
- Salt to taste
- Pepper to taste
- Garlic powder

- ➢ Onion powder
- ➢ Cayenne
- ➢ Paprika
- ➢ Seasoning salt
- ➢ Bbq sauce to taste

Preparation Method

1. Preheat the Green Mountain Grill to low.
2. In a mixing bowl, mix all the seasoning ingredients then toss the chicken wings until well coated.
3. Place the wings on the grill and cook for 20 minutes or until the wings are fully cooked.
4. Let rest to cool for 5 minutes then toss with bbq sauce.
5. Serve with orzo and salad. Enjoy.

Nutritional Information

Calories 311, Total fat 22g, Saturated fat 4g, Total carbs 22g, Net carbs 19g, Protein 22g, Sugar 12g, Fiber 3g, Sodium: 1400mg

Bacon-wrapped Chicken Tenders

These bacon-wrapped tenders are delicious, moist, and simply the best snack to carry in your snack box. If you want them more crispy broil them for a few more minutes until your desired crispness is achieved.
Prep time: 25 minutes, **Cook time:** 30 minutes; **Serves:** 6

Ingredients

1 lb chicken tenders
10 strips bacon
1/2 tbsp Italian seasoning
1/2 tbsp black pepper
1/2 tbsp salt
1 tbsp paprika
1 tbsp onion powder
1 tbsp garlic powder
1/3 cup light brown sugar
1 tbsp chili powder

Preparation Method

1. Preheat your wood pellet smoker to 350°F.
2. In a mixing bowl, mix Italian seasoning, black pepper, salt, paprika, onion, and garlic until well mixed.

3. Sprinkle the mixture on all sides of the chicken tenders and ensure they are well covered.
4. Wrap each chicken tender with a strip of bacon and tuck the ends.
5. Mix sugar and chili then sprinkle the mixture on the bacon-wrapped chicken.
6. Place them on the smoker and smoker for 30 minutes with the lid closed or until the chicken is cooked.
7. If you desire more crispiness, place the chicken on a baking sheet and broil for a few minutes.
8. Serve and enjoy.

Nutritional Information

Calories 206, Total fat 7.9g, Saturated fat 3.7g, Total Carbs 1.5g, Net Carbs 1.5g, Protein 30.3g, Sugar 1.5g, Fiber 0g, Sodium: 302mg

CHAPTER 5

Vegan and vegetarian Recipes

Grilled Mushrooms

If in search of a vegetarian side dish that is flavourful and easy to make, this Grilled mushrooms may steal the show.
Prep time: 15 minutes, **Cook time:** 45 minutes; **Serves:** 5

Ingredients

- 4 cup portobello, whole and cleaned
- 1 tbsp canola oil
- 1 tbsp onion powder
- 1 tbsp granulated garlic
- 1tbsp salt
- 1 tbsp pepper

Preparation Method

1. In a mixing bowl, add all the ingredients and mix well.
2. Set the wood pellet temperature to 180°F then place the mushrooms directly on the grill.
3. Smoke the mushrooms for 30 minutes.
4. Increase the temperature to high and cook the mushrooms for a further 15 minutes.
5. Serve and enjoy.

Nutritional Information

Calories 1680, Total fat 30g, Saturated fat 2g, Total Carbs 10g, Net Carbs 10g, Protein 4g, Sugar 0g, Fiber 0g, Sodium: 514mg, Potassium 0mg

Grilled Zucchini Squash Spears

This zucchini squash is a delicious vegetarian dish and a great way to elevate your veggie game. Serve them alongside your favorite side dish.
Prep time: 5 minutes, **Cook time:** 10 minutes; **Serves:** 5

Ingredients

- 4 zucchini, cleaned and ends cut
- 2 tbsp olive oil

- 1 tbsp sherry vinegar
- 2 thyme, leaves pulled
- Salt and pepper to taste

Preparation Method

1. Cut the zucchini into halves then cut each half thirds.
2. Add the rest of the ingredients in a ziplock bag with the zucchini pieces. Toss to mix well.
3. Preheat the wood pellet temperature to 350°F with the lid closed for 15 minutes.
4. Remove the zucchini from the bag and place them on the grill grate with the cut side down.
5. Cook for 4 minutes per side or until the zucchini are tender.
6. Remove from grill and serve with thyme leaves. Enjoy.

Nutritional Information

Calories 74, Total fat 5.4g, Saturated fat 0.5g, Total Carbs 6.1g, Net Carbs 3.8g, Protein 2.6g, Sugar 3.9g, Fiber 2.3g, Sodium: 302mg, Potassium 599mg

Whole Roasted Cauliflower with Garlic Parmesan Butter

Who said cauliflower has to be boring? This whole roasted cauliflower will surprise you with how awesome this vegetable can be.
Prep time: 15 minutes, **Cook time:** 45 minutes; **Serves:** 5

Ingredients

- 1/4 cup olive oil
- Salt and pepper to taste
- 1 cauliflower, fresh
- 1/2 cup butter, melted
- 1/4 cup parmesan cheese, grated
- 2 garlic cloves, minced
- 1/2 tbsp parsley, chopped

Preparation Method

1. Preheat the Green Mountain Grill with the lid closed for 15 minutes.
2. Meanwhile, brush the cauliflower with oil then season with salt and pepper.
3. Place the cauliflower in a cast iron and place it on a grill grate.
4. Cook for 45 minutes or until the cauliflower is golden brown and tender.
5. Meanwhile, mix butter, cheese, garlic, and parsley in a mixing bowl.
6. In the last 20 minutes of cooking, add the butter mixture.
7. Remove the cauliflower from the grill and top with more cheese and parsley if you desire. Enjoy.

Calories 156, Total fat 11.1g, Saturated fat 3.4g, Total Carbs 8.8g, Net Carbs 5.1g, Protein 8.2g, Sugar 0g, Fiber 3.7g, Sodium: 316mg, Potassium 468.2mg

Wood Pellet Cold Grilled Cheese

This cold-Grilled cheese is a perfect snack when served with crackers, pickled vegetables, or wine. This is a must-try in your new Green Mountain Grill.
Prep time: 5 minutes, **Cook time:** 2 minutes; **Serves:** 10

Ingredients

- Ice
- 1 aluminum pan, full-size and disposable
- 1 aluminum pan, half-size and disposable
- Toothpicks
- A block of cheese

Preparation Method

1. Preheat the wood pellet to 165°F wit the lid closed for 15 minutes.
2. Place the small pan in the large pan. Fill the surrounding of the small pan with ice.
3. Place the cheese in the small pan on top of toothpicks then place the pan on the grill and close the lid.
4. Smoke cheese for 1 hour, flip the cheese, and smoke for 1 more hour with the lid closed.
5. Remove the cheese from the grill and wrap it in parchment paper. Store in the fridge for 2 3 days for the smoke flavor to mellow.
6. Remove from the fridge and serve. Enjoy.

Nutritional Information

Calories 1910, Total fat 7g, Saturated fat 6g, Total Carbs 2g, Net Carbs 2g, Protein 6g, Sugar 1g, Fiber 0g, Sodium: 340mg, Potassium 0mg

Grilled Asparagus and Honey Glazed Carrots

This is a delicious grilled and glazed vegetable recipe that is perfect for vegetarians and vegans. This recipe takes your vegetable side dish to the next level.
Prep time: 15 minutes, **Cook time:** 35 minutes; **Serves:** 5

Ingredients

- 1 bunch asparagus, trimmed ends
- 1 lb carrots, peeled
- 2 tbsp olive oil
- Sea salt to taste
- 2 tbsp honey
- Lemon zest

Preparation Method

1. Sprinkle the asparagus with oil and sea salt. Drizzle the carrots with honey and salt.
2. Preheat the wood pellet to 165°F wit the lid closed for 15 minutes.
3. Place the carrots in the wood pellet and cook for 15 minutes. Add asparagus and cook for 20 more minutes or until cooked through.
4. Top the carrots and asparagus with lemon zest. Enjoy.

Nutritional Information

Calories 1680, Total fat 30g, Saturated fat 2g, Total Carbs 10g, Net Carbs 10g, Protein 4g, Sugar 0g, Fiber 0g, Sodium: 514mg, Potassium 0mg

Grilled Deviled Eggs

Are you looking for a crowd-pleasing appetizer for your vegetarian friends? These deviled eggs are the best choice.
Prep time: 15 minutes, **Cook time:** 30 minutes; **Serves:** 5

Ingredients

- 7 hard-boiled eggs, peeled
- 3 tbsp mayonnaise
- 3 tbsp chives, diced
- 1 tbsp brown mustard
- 1 tbsp apple cider vinegar
- Dash of hot sauce
- Salt and pepper
- 2 tbsp cooked bacon, crumbled
- Paprika to taste

Preparation Method

1. Preheat the wood pellet to 180°F for 15 minutes with the lid closed.
2. Place the eggs on the grill grate and smoke the eggs for 30 minutes. Remove the eggs from the grill and let cool.

3. Half the eggs and scoop the egg yolks into a zip lock bag.
4. Add all other ingredients in the zip lock bag except bacon and paprika. Mix until smooth.
5. Pipe the mixture into the egg whites then top with bacon and paprika.
6. Let rest then serve and enjoy.

Nutritional Information

Calories 140, Total fat 12g, Saturated fat 3g, Total Carbs 1g, Net Carbs 1g, Protein 6g, Sugar 0g, Fiber 0g, Sodium: 210mg, Potassium 100mg

Grilled Vegetables

If you are looking for a great way to deal with party leftovers, then this is a definite winner.
Prep time: 5 minutes, **Cook time:** 15 minutes; **Serves:** 8

Ingredients

➢ 1 veggie tray
➢ 1/4 cup vegetable oil
➢ 2 tbsp veggie seasoning

Preparation Method

1. Preheat the Green Mountain Grill to 375°F
2. Toss the vegetables in oil then place on a sheet pan.
3. Sprinkle with veggie seasoning then place on the hot grill.
4. Grill for 15 minutes or until the veggies are cooked.
5. Let rest then serve. Enjoy.

Nutritional Information

Calories 44, Total fat 5g, Saturated fat 0g, Total Carbs 1g, Net Carbs 1g, Protein 0g, Sugar 0g, Fiber 0g, Sodium: 36mg, Potassium 10mg

Grilled Asparagus

Asparagus is a popular vegetable that is packed with nutrients and a staple for vegetarians. You can now add a kick of the asparagus flavor by smoking it in the wood pellet.
Prep time: 5 minutes, **Cook time:** 1 hour; **Serves:** 4

Ingredients

- 1 bunch fresh asparagus, ends cut
- 2 tbsp olive oil
- Salt and pepper to taste

Preparation Method

1. Fire up your wood pellet smoker to 230°F
2. Place the asparagus in a mixing bowl and drizzle with olive oil. Season with salt and pepper.
3. Place the asparagus in a tinfoil sheet and fold the sides such that you create a basket.
4. Smoke the asparagus for 1 hour or until soft turning after half an hour.
5. Remove from the grill and serve. Enjoy.

Nutritional Information

Calories 43, Total fat 2g, Saturated fat 0g, Total Carbs 4g, Net Carbs 2g, Protein 3g, Sugar 2g, Fiber 2g, Sodium: 148mg

Grilled Acorn Squash

This acorn squash is a perfect vegetarian main dish or a welcome side dish that you can serve your family or friends. It can also be added into soups and stews for a hearty dish.

Prep time: 10 minutes, **Cook time:** 2 hours; **Serves:** 6

Ingredients

- 3 tbsp olive oil
- 3 acorn squash, halved and seeded
- 1/4 cup unsalted butter
- 1/4 cup brown sugar
- 1 tbsp cinnamon, ground
- 1 tbsp chili powder
- 1 tbsp nutmeg, ground

Preparation Method

1. Brush olive oil on the acorn squash cut sides then cover the halves with foil. Poke holes on the foil to allow steam and smoke through.
2. Fire up the wood pellet to 225°F and smoke the squash for 1 ½-2 hours.
3. Remove the squash from the smoker and allow it to sit.
4. Meanwhile, melt butter, sugar and spices in a saucepan. Stir well to combine.
5. Remove the foil from the squash and spoon the butter mixture in each squash half. Enjoy.

Calories 149, Total fat 10g, Saturated fat 5g, Total Carbs 14g, Net Carbs 12g, Protein 2g, Sugar 0g, Fiber 2g, Sodium: 19mg, Potassium 0mg

Vegan Grilled Carrot Dogs

If you a lover of hot dogs but want to keep it vegetarian or vegan this is a perfect swap.
Prep time: 25 minutes, **Cook time:** 35 minutes; **Serves:** 4

Ingredients

- 4 thick carrots
- 2 tbsp avocado oil
- 1 tbsp liquid smoke
- 1/2 tbsp garlic powder
- Salt and pepper to taste

Preparation Method

1. Preheat the Green Mountain Grill to 425°F and line a baking sheet with parchment paper.
2. Peel the carrots and round the edges.
3. In a mixing bowl, mix oil, liquid smoke, garlic, salt, and pepper. Place the carrots on the baking dish then pour the mixture over.
4. Roll the carrots to coat evenly with the mixture and use fingertips to massage the mixture into the carrots.
5. Place in the grill and grill for 35 minutes or until the carrots are fork-tender ensuring to turn and brush the carrots every 5 minutes with the marinade.
6. Remove from the grill and place the carrots in hot dog bun. Serve with your favorite toppings and enjoy.

Nutritional Information

Calories 149, Total fat 1.6g, Saturated fat 0.3g, Total Carbs 27.9g, Net Carbs 24.3g, Protein 5.4g, Sugar 5.6g, Fiber 3.6g, Sodium: 516mg, Potassium 60mg

Grilled Vegetables

These veggies are a sure show stoppers. Heating the wet wood pellets gives a smokey and savory flavor that is impacted in the veggies making the insanely delicious.

Prep time: 5 minutes, **Cook time:** 15 minutes; **Serves:** 6

Ingredients

- ➢ 1 ear corn, fresh, husks and silk strands removed
- ➢ 1yellow squash, sliced
- ➢ 1 red onion, cut into wedges
- ➢ 1 green pepper, cut into strips
- ➢ 1 red pepper, cut into strips
- ➢ 1 yellow pepper, cut into strips
- ➢ 1 cup mushrooms, halved
- ➢ 2 tbsp oil
- ➢ 2 tbsp chicken seasoning

Preparation Method

1. Soak the pecan wood pellets in water for an hour. Remove the pellets from water and fill the smoker box with the wet pellets.
2. Place the smoker box under the grill and close the lid. Heat the grill on high heat for 10 minutes or until smoke starts coming out from the wood chips.
3. Meanwhile, toss the veggies in oil and seasonings then transfer them into a grill basket.
4. Grill for 10 minutes while turning occasionally. Serve and enjoy.

Nutritional Information

Calories 97, Total fat 5g, Saturated fat 2g, Total Carbs 11g, Net Carbs 8g, Protein 2g, Sugar 1g, Fiber 3g, Sodium: 251mg, Potassium 171mg

Wood Pellet Grill Spicy Sweet Potatoes

This is a delicious crowd pleaser vegan dish that everyone will love. The spicy-sweet potatoes leave the taste buds rejoicing and asking for more.
Prep time: 10 minutes,
Cook time: 35 minutes; **Serves:** 6

Ingredients

- ➢ 2 lb sweet potatoes, cut into chunks
- ➢ 1 red onion, chopped
- ➢ 2 tbsp oil
- ➢ 2 tbsp orange juice
- ➢ 1 tbsp roasted cinnamon
- ➢ 1 tbsp salt
- ➢ 1/4 tbsp Chiptole chili pepper

Preparation Method

1. Preheat the Green Mountain Grill to 425°F with the lid closed.
2. Toss the sweet potatoes with onion, oil, and juice.
3. In a mixing bowl, mix cinnamon, salt, and pepper then sprinkle the mixture over the sweet potatoes.
4. Spread the potatoes on a lined baking dish in a single layer.
5. Place the baking dish in the grill and grill for 30 minutes or until the sweet potatoes ate tender.
6. Serve and enjoy.

Nutritional Information

Calories 145, Total fat 5g, Saturated fat 0g, Total Carbs 23g, Net Carbs 19g, Protein 2g, Sugar 3g, Fiber 4g, Sodium: 428mg, Potassium 230mg

Grilled Stuffed Zucchini

These Stuffed zucchini are all you need during snack time. They are healthy, easy to make, delicious and can be eaten by everyone.
Prep time: 5 minutes,
Cook time: 11 minutes; **Serves:** 8

Ingredients

- ➤ 4 zucchini
- ➤ 5 tbsp olive oil
- ➤ 2 tbsp red onion, chopped
- ➤ 1/4 tbsp garlic, minced
- ➤ 1/2 cup bread crumbs
- ➤ 1/2 cup mozzarella cheese, shredded
- ➤ 1 tbsp fresh mint
- ➤ 1/2 tbsp salt
- ➤ 3 tbsp parmesan cheese

Preparation Method

1. Cut the zucchini lengthwise and scoop out the pulp then brush the shells with oil.
2. In a non-stick skillet sauté pulp, onion, and remaining oil. Add garlic and cook for a minute.
3. Add bread crumbs and cook until golden brown. Remove from heat and stir in mozzarella cheese, fresh mint, and salt.
4. Spoon the mixture into the shells and sprinkle parmesan cheese.
5. Place in a grill and grill for 10 minutes or until the zucchini are tender.

Nutritional Information

Calories 186, Total fat 10g, Saturated fat 5g, Total Carbs 17g, Net Carbs 14g, Protein 9g, Sugar 4g, Fiber 3g, Sodium: 553mg

Grilled Mexican Street Corn

This is a yummy and easy side dish to serve your vegetarian friends. It's easy to make and infused with flavors in the wood pellet.

Prep time: 5 minutes, **Cook time:** 25 minutes; **Serves:** 6

Ingredients

- 6 ears of corn on the cob, shucked
- 1 tbsp olive oil
- Kosher salt and pepper to taste
- 1/4 cup mayo
- 1/4 cup sour cream
- 1 tbsp garlic paste
- 1/2 tbsp chili powder
- Pinch of ground red pepper
- 1/2 cup cotija cheese, crumbled
- 1/4 cup cilantro, chopped
- 6 lime wedges

Preparation Method

1. Brush the corn with oil and sprinkle with salt.
2. Place the corn on a Green Mountain Grill set at 350°F. Cook for 25 minutes as you turn it occasionally.
3. Meanwhile mix mayo, cream, garlic, chili, and red pepper until well combined.
4. When the corn is cooked remove from the grill, let it rest for some minutes then brush with the mayo mixture.
5. Sprinkle cotija cheese, more chili powder, and cilantro. Serve with lime wedges. Enjoy.

Nutritional Information

Calories 144, Total fat 5g, Saturated fat 2g, Total Carbs 10g, Net Carbs 10g, Protein 0g, Sugar 0g, Fiber 0g, Sodium: 136mg, Potassium 173mg

Wood Pellet Bacon Wrapped Jalapeno Poppers

These delicious and easy jalapeno poppers are packed with cheese and grilled for perfection. It's simply the best brunch to carry in your snack box to work.
Prep time: 10 minutes, **Cook time:** 20 minutes; **Serves:** 6

Ingredients

- ➤ 6 jalapenos, fresh
- ➤ 4 oz cream cheese
- ➤ 1/2 cup cheddar cheese, shredded
- ➤ 1 tbsp vegetable rub
- ➤ 12 slices cut bacon

Preparation Method

1. Preheat the wood pellet smoker and grill to375°F.
2. Slice the jalapenos lengthwise and scrape the seed and membrane. Rinse them with water and set aside.
3. In a mixing bowl, mix cream cheese, cheddar cheese, vegetable rub until well mixed.
4. Fill the jalapeno halves with the mixture then wrap with the bacon pieces.
5. Smoke for 20 minutes or until the bacon crispy.
6. Serve and enjoy.

Nutritional Information

Calories 1830, Total fat 11g, Saturated fat 6g, Total Carbs 5g, Net Carbs 4g, Protein 6g, Sugar 4g, Fiber 1g

CHAPTER 6

Grilled salmon

If you are a lover of salmon, you will be amazed at how flavourful home-Grilled salmon can be. It's also very easy to make in your wood pellet smoker and grill.
Prep time: 10 minutes, **Cook time:** 4 hours; **Serves:** 8

Ingredients

Brine
➢ 4 cups water
➢ 1 cup brown sugar
➢ 1/3 cup kosher salt

Salmon
➢ Salmon fillet, skin in
➢ Maple syrup

Preparation Method

1. Combine all the brine ingredients until the sugar has fully dissolved.
2. Add the brine to a ziplock bag with the salmon and refrigerate for 12 hours.
3. Remove the salmon from the brine, wash it and rinse with water. Pat dry with paper towel then let sit at room temperature for 2 hours.
4. Startup your wood pellet to smoke and place the salmon on a baking rack sprayed with cooking spray.
5. After cooking for an hour, baste the salmon with maple syrup. Do not let the smoker get above 180°F for accurate results.
6. Smoke for 3-4 hours or until the salmon flakes easily.

Nutritional Information

Calories 101, Total fat 2g, Saturated fat 0g, Total carbs 16g, Net carbs 16g, Protein 4g, Sugar 16g, Fiber 0g, Sodium: 3131mg

Wood Pellet Teriyaki Grilled Shrimp

Honestly, this is one of my favorite and quickest dinners. I love the way this Grilled shrimp is easy to make yet very fancy.
Prep time: 10 minutes, **Cook time:** 10 minutes; **Serves:** 6

Ingredients

- 1 lb tail-on shrimp, uncooked
- 1/2 tbsp onion powder
- 1/2 tbsp salt
- 1/2 tbsp Garlic powder
- 4 tbsp Teriyaki sauce
- 4 tbsp sriracha mayo
- 2 tbsp green onion, minced

Preparation Method

1. Peel the shrimps leaving the tails then wash them removing any vein left over. Drain and pat with a paper towel to drain.
2. Preheat the wood pellet to 450°F
3. Season the shrimp with onion, salt, and garlic then place it on the grill to cook for 5 minutes on each side.
4. Remove the shrimp from the grill and toss it with teriyaki sauce. Serve garnished with mayo and onions. Enjoy.

Nutritional Information

Calories 87, Total fat 0g, Saturated fat 0g, Total Carbs 2g, Net Carbs 2g, Protein 16g, Sugar 1g, Fiber 0g, Sodium: 1241mg

Grilled Scallops

These are easy to make scallops that get a smokey touch from the wood pellets and stay tender by cooking in butter on a cast iron.
Prep time: 5 minutes, **Cook time:** 15 minutes; **Serves:** 4

Ingredients

- 2 lb sea scallops, dried with a paper towel
- 1/2 tbsp garlic salt
- 2 tbsp kosher salt
- 4 tbsp salted butter
- Squeeze lemon juice

Preparation Method

1. Preheat the Green Mountain Grill to 400°F with the cast pan inside.
2. Sprinkle with both salts, pepper on both sides of the scallops.
3. Place the butter on the cast iron then add the scallops. Close the lid and cook for 8 minutes.
4. Flip the scallops and close the lid once more. Cook for 8 more minutes.

5. Remove the scallops from the grill and give a lemon squeeze. Serve immediately and enjoy.

Nutritional Information

Calories 177, Total fat 7g, Saturated fat 4g, Total Carbs 6g, Net Carbs 6g, Protein 23g, Sugar 0g, Fiber 0g, Sodium: 1430mg, Potassium 359mg

Grilled Shrimp Scampi

Why should you heat up your house in summer while you can enjoy this smokey flavored Grilled Shrimp Scampi
Prep time: 5 minutes, **Cook time:** 10 minutes; **Serves:** 4

Ingredients

- ➢ 1 lb raw shrimp, tail on
- ➢ 1/2 cup salted butter, melted
- ➢ 1/4 cup white wine, dry
- ➢ 1/2 tbsp fresh garlic, chopped
- ➢ 1 tbsp lemon juice
- ➢ 1/2 tbsp garlic powder
- ➢ 1/2 tbsp salt

Preparation Method

1. Preheat your Green Mountain Grill to 400°F with a cast iron inside.
2. In a mixing bowl, mix butter, wine, garlic, and juice then pour in the cast iron. Let the mixture mix for 4 minutes.
3. Sprinkle garlic and salt on the shrimp then place it on the cast iron. Grill for 10 minutes with the lid closed.
4. Remove the shrimp from the grill and serve when hot. Enjoy.

Nutritional Information

Calories 298, Total fat 24g, Saturated fat 15g, Total Carbs 2g, Net Carbs 2g, Protein 16g, Sugar 0g, Fiber 0g, Sodium: 1091mg, Potassium 389mg

Grilled Buffalo Shrimp

This awesome Grilled buffalo shrimp is tender, has a smoke touch and the buffalo sauce gives it a spicy wonder. You will want to make this recipe over and over again.
Prep time: 10 minutes, **Cook time:** 5 minutes; **Serves:** 6

Ingredients

- 1 lb raw shrimps peeled and deveined
- 1/2 tbsp salt
- 1/4 tbsp garlic salt
- 1/4 tbsp garlic powder
- 1/4 tbsp onion powder
- 1/2 cup buffalo sauce

Preparation Method

1. Preheat the Green Mountain Grill to 450°F.
2. Coat the shrimp with both salts, garlic and onion powders.
3. Place the shrimp in a grill and cook for 3 minutes on each side.
4. Remove from the grill and toss in buffalo sauce. Serve with cheese, celery and napkins. Enjoy.

Nutritional Information

Calories 57, Total fat 1g, Saturated fat 0g, Total Carbs 1g, Net Carbs 1g, Protein 10g, Sugar 0g, Fiber 0g, Sodium: 1106mg, Potassium 469mg

Grilled Salmon Sandwich

These delicious and tender salmon sandwiches are made with grilled salmon topped with butter lettuce and aioli.

Prep time: 10 minutes, **Cook time:** 15 minutes; **Serves:** 4

Ingredients

Salmon Sandwiches
- 4 salmon fillets
- 1 tbsp olive oil
- Fin and feather rub
- 1 tbsp salt
- 4 toasted bun
- Butter lettuce

Dill Aioli
- 1/2 cup mayonnaise
- 1/2 tbsp lemon zest
- 2 tbsp lemon juice
- 1/4 tbsp salt
- 1/2 tbsp fresh dill, minced

Preparation Method

1. Mix all the dill aioli ingredients and place them in the fridge.
2. Preheat the Green Mountain Grill to 450°F.
3. Brush the salmon fillets with oil, rub, and salt. Place the fillets on the grill and cook until the internal temperature reaches 135°F.
4. Remove the fillets from the grill and let rest for 5 minutes.
5. Spread the aioli on the buns then top with salmon, lettuce, and the top bun.
6. Serve when hot.

Nutritional Information

Calories 852, Total fat 54g, Saturated fat 10g, Total Carbs 30g, Net Carbs 28g, Protein 57g, Sugar 5g, Fiber 2g, Sodium: 1268mg, Potassium 379mg

Grilled Teriyaki salmon

This is a savory, easy, and healthy dinner meal that every member of your family will love and ask for more.
Prep time: 10 minutes, **Cook time:** 30 minutes; **Serves:** 4

Ingredients

- 1 salmon fillet
- 1/8 cup olive oil
- 1/2 tbsp salt
- 1/4 tbsp pepper
- 1/4 tbsp garlic salt
- 1/4 cup butter, sliced
- 1/4 teriyaki sauce
- 1 tbsp sesame seeds

Preparation Method

1. Preheat the grill to 400°F.
2. Place the salmon fillet on a non-stick foil sheet. Drizzle the salmon with oil, seasonings, and butter on top.
3. Pace the foil tray on the grill and close the lid. Cook for 8 minutes then open the lid.
4. Brush the salmon with teriyaki sauce and repeat after every 5 minutes until all sauce is finished. The internal temperature should be 145°F.
5. Remove the salmon from the grill and sprinkle with sesame seeds.
6. Serve and enjoy with your favorite side dish.

Nutritional Information

Calories 296, Total fat 25g, Saturated fat 10g, Total Carbs 3g, Net Carbs 3g, Protein 14g, Sugar 3g, Fiber 0g, Sodium: 1179mg, Potassium 459mg

Wood Pellet Togarashi Grilled Salmon

Do you love spicy salmon? This togarashi salmon is packed with a little kick from the spices and is very easy to make.

Prep time: 5 minutes, **Cook time:** 20 minutes; **Serves:** 6

Ingredients

1 salmon fillet
1/4 cup olive oil
1/2 tbsp kosher salt
1 tbsp Togarashi seasoning

Preparation Method

1. Preheat the Green Mountain Grill to 400°F.
2. Place the salmon fillet on a non-stick foil sheet with the skin side up.
3. Rub the olive oil on the salmon and sprinkle with salt and togarashi seasoning.
4. Place the salmon on the preheated grill and close the lid. Cook for 20 minutes or until the internal temperature reaches 145°F.
5. Remove from the grill and serve when hot. Enjoy.

Nutritional Information

Calories 119, Total fat 10g, Saturated fat 2g, Total Carbs 0g, Net Carbs 0g, Protein 6g, Sugar 0g, Fiber 0g, Sodium: 720mg

Grilled Lingcod

What more would you wish for on top of a delicious grilled lingcod that is packed with flavors from the crazy seasonings?

Prep time: 10 minutes, **Cook time:** 15 minutes; **Serves:** 6

Ingredients

- 2 lb lingcod fillets
- 1/2 tbsp salt
- 1/2 tbsp white pepper
- 1/4 tbsp cayenne
- Lemon wedges

Preparation Method

1. Preheat the Green Mountain Grill to 375°F.
2. Place the lingcod on a parchment paper and season it with salt, white pepper, cayenne pepper then top with the lemon.

3. Place the fish on the grill and cook for 15 minutes or until the internal temperature reaches 145°F.
4. Serve and enjoy.

Nutritional Information

Calories 245, Total fat 2g, Saturated fat 0g, Total Carbs 2g, Net Carbs 1g, Protein 52g, Sugar 1g, Fiber 1g, Sodium: 442mg, Potassium 649mg

Wood pellet Rockfish

The lemons with the simple seasonings make this wood pellet rockfish shine and win the golden ticket. You definitely need to try this awesome recipe.
Prep time: 10 minutes, **Cook time:** 20 minutes; **Serves:** 6

Ingredients

- 6 rockfish fillets
- 1 lemon, sliced
- 3/4 tbsp Himalayan salt
- 2 tbsp fresh dill, chopped
- 1/2 tbsp garlic powder
- 1/2 tbsp onion powder
- 6 tbsp butter

Preparation Method

1. Preheat your Green Mountain Grill to 375°F.
2. Place the rockfish in a baking dish and season with salt, dill, garlic, and onion.
3. Place butter on top of the fish then close the lid. Cook for 20 minutes or until the fish is no longer translucent.
4. Remove from grill and let sit for 5 minutes before serving. enjoy.

Nutritional Information

Calories 270, Total fat 17g, Saturated fat 9g, Total Carbs 2g, Net Carbs 0g, Protein 28g, Sugar 0g, Fiber 0g, Sodium: 381mg

Wood Pellet Salt and Pepper Spot Prawn Skewers

Do you love seafood and want to throw something new that is not beef or lamb in your wood pellet? These prawn skewers are the real deal.
Prep time: 10 minutes, **Cook time:** 10 minutes; **Serves:** 6

Ingredients

- ➤ 2 lb spot prawns, clean
- ➤ 2 tbsp oil
- ➤ Salt and pepper to taste

Preparation Method

1. Preheat your grill to 400°F.
2. Meanwhile, soak the skewers then skewer with the prawns.
3. Brush with oil then season with salt and pepper to taste.
4. Place the skewers in the grill, close the lid, and cook for 5 minutes on each side.
5. Remove from the grill and serve. Enjoy.

Nutritional Information

Calories 221, Total fat 7g, Saturated fat 1g, Total Carbs 2g, Net Carbs 2g, Protein 34g, Sugar 0g, Fiber 0g, Sodium: 1481mg, Potassium 239mg

Bacon-wrapped Shrimp

Are you in a fix of finding the perfect appetizer to serve in the upcoming family or friends gathering? Look no further. This is a solid choice.

Prep time: 20 minutes, **Cook time:** 10 minutes; **Serves:** 12

Ingredients

- ➤ 1 lb raw shrimp
- ➤ 1/2 tbsp salt
- ➤ 1/4 tbsp garlic powder
- ➤ 1 lb bacon, halved

Preparation Method

1. Preheat the Green Mountain Grill to 350°F.
2. Remove the tail shells on the shrimp placing them on a paper towel.
3. Season the shrimps with salt and garlic then wrap with bacon and secure with a toothpick.
4. Place the shrimps on a baking rack that is coated with cooking spray.
5. Cook for 10 minutes on each side or until you achieve your desired crispiness.
6. Remove from the grill and serve when hot. Enjoy.

Nutritional Information

Calories 204, Total fat 14g, Saturated fat 5g, Total Carbs 1g, Net Carbs 1g, Protein 18g, Sugar 0g, Fiber 0g, Sodium: 939mg, Potassium 474mg

Bacon-wrapped Scallops

These are simple bacon wrapped scallops that are delicious, crispy, and tender. They make a perfect crowd-pleasing appetizer.

Prep time: 15 minutes, **Cook time:** 20 minutes; **Serves:** 8

Ingredients

- ➢ 1 lb sea scallops
- ➢ 1/2 lb bacon
- ➢ Salt to taste

Preparation Method

1. Preheat your Green Mountain Grill to 375°F.
2. Pat dry the scallops with paper towel then wrap with the bacon and secure with a toothpick.
3. Lay the scallops on the grill with the bacon side down. Close the lid and cook for 7 minutes on each side.
4. The bacon should be crispy and scallops tender. Remove from the grill and serve. Enjoy.

Nutritional Information

Calories 261, Total fat 14g, Saturated fat 5g, Total Carbs 5g, Net Carbs 5g, Protein 28g, Sugar 0g, Fiber 0g, Sodium: 1238mg, Potassium 559mg

Grilled Lobster Tail

This is a surprisingly delicious special dinner that is fast and easy to make in your wood pellet.you will not want to miss on the best way to use shellfish.

Prep time: 10 minutes, **Cook time:** 15 minutes; **Serves:** 2

Ingredients

- ➢ 10 oz lobster tail
- ➢ 1/4 tbsp old bay seasoning
- ➢ 1/4 tbsp Himalayan sea salt
- ➢ 2 tbsp butter, melted
- ➢ 1 tbsp fresh parsley, chopped

Preparation Method

1. Preheat the wood pellet to 450°F.
2. Slice the tails down the middle using a knife.
3. Season with seasoning and salt then place the tails on the grill grate.
4. Grill for 15 minutes or until the internal temperature reaches 140°F..
5. Remove the tails and drizzle with butter and garnish with parsley.
6. Serve and enjoy.

Nutritional Information

Calories 305, Total fat 14g, Saturated fat 8g, Total Carbs 5g, Net Carbs 5g, Protein 18g, Sugar 0g, Fiber 0g, Sodium: 685mg, Potassium 159mg

Wood Pellet Garlic Dill Grilled Salmon

This is an outstanding appetizer that will blow everyone's mind and they will ask for more. The salmon is brined then grilled on the wood pellet giving it an irresistibly sweet taste

Prep time: 15minutes, **Cook time:** 4 hours; **Serves:** 12

Ingredients

➢ 2 salmon fillets

Brine

➢ 4 cups water
➢ 1 cup brown sugar
➢ 1/3 cup kosher salt

Seasoning

➢ 3 tbsp minced garlic
➢ 1 tbsp fresh dill, chopped

Preparation Method

1. In a zip lock bag, combine the brine ingredients until all sugar has dissolved. Place the salmon in the bag and refrigerate overnight.
2. Remove the salmon from the brine, rinse with water and pat dry with a paper towel. Let it rest for 2-4 hours at room temperature.
3. Season the salmon with garlic and dill generously.
4. Fire up the Green Mountain Grill to smoke and place the salmon on a cooling rack that is coated with cooking spray.
5. Place the rack in the smoker and close the lid.
6. Smoke the salmon for 4 hours until the smoke is between 130-180°F.
7. Remove the salmon from the grill and serve with crackers. Enjoy

Nutritional Information

Calories 139, Total fat 5g, Saturated fat 1g, Total Carbs 16g, Net Carbs 16g, Protein 9g, Sugar 0g, Fiber 0g, Sodium: 3143mg

CHAPTER 7

Grilled Carrots

This is an easy side dish prepared on the Green Mountain Grill. These grilled carrots are delicious, flavored by fresh herbs, browned butter and the grill.
Prep time: 5 minutes, **Cook time:** 20 minutes; **Serves** 6

Ingredients

- 1 lb carrots, large
- 1/2 tbsp salt
- 6 oz butter
- 1/2 tbsp black pepper
- Fresh thyme

Preparation Method

1. Thoroughly wash the carrots and do not peel. Pat them dry and coat with olive oil.
2. Add salt to your carrots.
3. Meanwhile, preheat a pellet grill to 350°F.
4. Now place your carrots directly on the grill or on a raised rack.
5. Close and cook for about 20 minutes.
6. While carrots cook, cook butter in a saucepan, small, over medium heat until browned. Stir constantly to avoid it from burning. Remove from heat.
7. Remove carrots from the grill onto a plate then drizzle with browned butter.
8. Add pepper and splash with thyme.
9. Serve and enjoy.

Nutritional Information

Calories 250, Total fat 25g, Saturated fat 15g, Total Carbs 6g, Net Carbs 4g, Protein 1g, Sugars 3g, Fiber 2g, Sodium 402mg, Potassium 369mg

Grilled Brussels Sprouts

These are bacon-tossed vegetables that you will love. The grilled Brussels sprouts are crispy and a perfect side dish for any main course.
Prep time: 15 minutes, **Cook time:** 20 minutes; **Serves** 8

Ingredients

- 1/2 lb bacon, grease reserved
- 1 lb Brussels Sprouts
- 1/2 tbsp pepper
- 1/2 tbsp salt

Preparation Method

1. Cook bacon until crispy on a stovetop, reserve its grease then chop into small pieces.
2. Meanwhile, wash the Brussels sprouts, trim off the dry end and remove dried leaves if any. Half them and set aside.
3. Place 1/4 cup reserved grease in a pan, cast-iron, over medium-high heat.
4. Season the Brussels sprouts with pepper and salt.
5. Brown the sprouts on the pan with the cut side down for about 3-4 minutes.
6. In the meantime, preheat your pellet grill to 350-375°F.
7. Place bacon pieces and browned sprouts into your grill-safe pan.
8. Cook for about 20 minutes. Serve immediately.

Nutritional Information

Calories 153, Total fat 10g, Saturated fat 3g, Total Carbs 5g, Net Carbs 3g, Protein 11g, Sugars 1g, Fiber 2g, Sodium 622mg, Potassium 497mg

Wood pellet Spicy Brisket

Serve this mouthwatering brisket alongside your favourite side and veggies for dinner meal.
Prep time: 20 minutes, **Cook time:** 9 hours; **Serves:** 10

Ingredients

- 2 tbsp garlic powder
- 2 tbsp onion powder
- 2 tbsp paprika
- 2 tbsp chili powder
- 1/3 cup salt
- 1/3 cup black pepper
- 12 lb whole packer brisket, trimmed
- 1-1/2 cup beef broth

Preparation Method

1. Set your wood pellet temperature to 225°F. Let preheat for 15 minutes with the lid closed.
2. Meanwhile, mix garlic, onion, paprika, chili, salt, and pepper in a mixing bowl.

3. the brisket generously on all sides.
4. Place the meat on the grill with the fat side down and let it cool until the internal temperature reaches 160°F.
5. Remove the meat from the grill and double wrap it with foil. Return it to the grill and cook until the internal temperature reaches 204°F.
6. Remove from grill, unwrap the brisket and let rest for 15 minutes.
7. Slice and serve.

Nutritional Information

Calories 270, Total fat 20g, Saturated fat 8g, Total Carbs 3g, Net Carbs 3g, Protein 20g, Sugar 1g, Fiber 0g, Sodium: 1220mg

Pellet Grill Funeral Potatoes

This is a classic side dish that everyone will go for on a holiday buffet or on a table. They are cheesy, and super easy to make.
Prep time: 10 minutes, **Cook time:** 1 hour; **Serves** 8

Ingredients

- ➤ 1, 32 oz, package frozen hash browns
- ➤ 1/2 cup cheddar cheese, grated
- ➤ 1 can cream of chicken soup
- ➤ 1 cup sour cream
- ➤ 1 cup Mayonnaise
- ➤ 3 cups corn flakes, whole or crushed
- ➤ 1/4 cup melted butter

Preparation Method

1. Preheat your pellet grill to 350°F.
2. Spray a 13 x 9 baking pan, aluminum, using a cooking spray, non-stick.
3. Mix together hash browns, cheddar cheese, chicken soup cream, sour cream, and mayonnaise in a bowl, large.
4. Spoon the mixture into a baking pan gently.
5. Mix corn flakes and melted butter then sprinkle over the casserole.
6. Grill for about 1-1½ hours until potatoes become tender. If the top browns too much, cover using a foil until potatoes are done.
7. Remove from the grill and serve hot.

Nutritional Information

Calories 403, Total fat 37g, Saturated fat 12g, Total Carbs 14g, Net Carbs 14g, Protein 4g, Sugars 2g, Fiber 0g, Sodium 620mg, Potassium 501mg

Smoky Caramelized Onions on the Pellet Grill

Do you love caramelized onions? Try making them on a Green Mountain Grill. The wood will provide the onions with a smoky layer making it delicious and perfect.
Prep time: 5 minutes, **Cook time:** 1 hour; **Serves** 4

Ingredients

- 5 large sliced onions
- 1/2 cup fat of your choice
- Pinch of Sea salt

Preparation Method

1. Place all the ingredients into a pan. For a deep rich brown caramelized onion, cook them off for about 1hour on a stovetop.
2. Keep the grill temperatures not higher than 250 - 275°F.
3. Now transfer the pan into the grill.
4. Cook for about 1-1½ hours until brown in color. Check and stir with a spoon, wooden, after every 15 minutes. Make sure not to run out of pellets.
5. Now remove from the grill and season with more salt if necessary.
6. Serve immediately or place in a refrigerator for up to 1 week.

Nutritional Information

Calories 286, Total fat 25.8g, Saturated fat 10.3g, Total Carbs 12.8g, Net Carbs 9.8g, Protein 1.5g, Sugars 5.8g, Fiber 3g Sodium 6mg, Potassium 201mg

Hickory Grilled Green Beans

Green beans come with a wonderful taste when prepared in a wood pellet smoker. It is a classic side dish full of flavor and perfect for any barbeque.
Prep time: 15 minutes, **Cook time:** 3 hours; **Serves** 10

Ingredients

- 6 cups fresh green beans, halved and ends cut off
- 2 cups chicken broth
- 1 tbsp pepper, ground
- 1/4 tbsp salt
- 2 tbsp apple cider vinegar
- 1/4 cup diced onion
- 6-8 bite-size bacon slices
- **Optional:** sliced almonds

Preparation Method

1. Add green beans to a colander then rinse well. Set aside.
2. Place chicken broth, pepper, salt, and apple cider in a pan, large. Add green beans.
3. Blanch over medium heat for about 3-4 minutes then remove from heat.
4. Transfer the mixture into an aluminum pan, disposable. Make sure all mixture goes into the pan so do not drain them.
5. Place bacon slices over the beans and place the pan into the wood pellet smoker,
6. Smoke for about 3 hours uncovered.
7. Remove from the smoker and top with almonds slices.
8. Serve immediately.

Nutritional Information

Calories 57, Total fat 3g, Saturated fat 1g, Total Carbs 6g, Net Carbs 4g, Protein 4g, Sugars 2g, Fiber 2g, Sodium 484mg, Potassium 216mg

Grilled Corn on the Cob

The best way to make a corn on the cob most flavorful is on a wood pellet smoker. This is a delicious side dish perfect for your steak or burgers and best for summertime. **Prep time:** 5 minutes, **Cook time:** 1 hour; **Serves** 4

Ingredients

- ➢ 4 corn ears, husk removed
- ➢ 4 tbsp olive oil
- ➢ Pepper and salt to taste

Preparation Method

1. Preheat your smoker to 225°F.
2. Meanwhile, brush your corn with olive oil. Season with pepper and salt.
3. Place the corn on a smoker and smoke for about 1 hour 15 minutes.
4. Remove from the smoker and serve.
5. Enjoy!

Nutritional Information

Calories 180, Total fat 7g, Saturated fat 4g, Total Carbs 31g, Net Carbs 27g, protein 5g, Sugars 5g, Fiber 4g, Sodium 23mg, Potassium 416mg

Grilled Vegetables

Grilled vegetables are very simple to prepare because they only require a very short time to cook. It is a simple side dish that all the family and friends will thank love.
Prep time: 5 minutes, **Cook time:** 20 minutes; **Serves** 4

Ingredients

- 1 head of broccoli
- 4 carrots
- 16 oz snow peas
- 1 tbsp olive oil
- 1 cup mushrooms, chopped
- 1-1/2 tbsp pepper
- 1 tbsp garlic powder

Preparation Method

1. Cut broccoli and carrots into bite-size pieces. Add snow peas and combine.
2. Toss the veggies with oil and seasoning.
3. Now cover a pan, sheet, with parchment paper. Place veggies on top.
4. Meanwhile, set your wood pellet smoker to 180°F.
5. Place the pan into the smoker. Smoke for about 5 minutes.
6. Adjust smoker temperature to 400°F and continue cooking for another 10-15 minutes until slightly brown broccoli tips.
7. Remove, Serve and enjoy.

Nutritional Information

Calories 111, Total fat 4g, Saturated fat 1g, Total Carbs 15g, Net Carbs 9g, Protein 5g, Sugars 7g, Fiber 6g, Sodium 0mg, Potassium 109mg

Easy Grilled Corn

This is truly and honestly the easiest grilled corn to prepare. It is a great side dish and once you grill, trust me you will never get back to boiling corn.
Prep time: 5 minutes, **Cook time:** 40 minutes; **Serves** 6

Ingredients

- 6 fresh corn ears, still in the husk
- Pepper, salt and butter

Preparation Method

1. Preheat your Green Mountain Grill to 375-400°F.

2. Cut off the large silk ball from the corn top and any hanging or loose husk pieces.
3. Place the corn on your grill grate directly and do not peel off the husk.
4. Grill for about 30-40 minutes. Flip a few times to grill evenly all round.
5. Transfer the corn on a platter, serve, and let guests peel their own.
6. Now top with pepper, salt and butter.
7. Enjoy!

Nutritional Information

Calories 77, Total fat 1g, Saturated fat 1g, Total carbs 17g, Net carbs 15g, Protein 3g, Sugars 6g, Fiber 2g, Sodium 14mg, Potassium 243mg

Seasoned Potatoes on Smoker

This is a quick and easy side dish recipe on a Green Mountain Grill. These crispy creamer potatoes are seasoned with parsley, thyme, oregano, and garlic making it full of flavor.
Prep time: 10 minutes, **Cook time:** 45 minutes; **Serves** 6

Ingredients

- 1-1/2 lb creamer potatoes
- 2 tbsp olive oil
- 1 tbsp garlic powder
- 1/4 tbsp oregano
- 1/2 tbsp thyme, dried
- 1/2 tbsp parsley, dried

Preparation Method

1. Preheat your pellet grill to 350°F.
2. Spray an 8x8 inch foil pan using non-stick spray.
3. Mix all ingredients in the pan and place it into the grill.
4. Cook for about 45 minutes until potatoes are done. Stir after every 15 minutes.
5. Serve and enjoy!

Nutritional Information

Calories 130, Total fat 4g, Saturated fat 2g, Total Carbs 20g, Net Carbs 18g, Protein 2g, Sugars 2g, Fiber 2g, Sodium 7mg, Potassium 483mg

CHAPTER 8

Cheese, Nuts, Breads and Desserts

Grilled Pumpkin Pie

Looking for a thanksgiving dessert? This Grilled pumpkin pie is easy and quick with a Grilled flavor which makes it amazing.
Prep time: 10 minutes, **Cook time:** 50 minutes; **Serves** 8

Ingredients

1. 1 tbsp cinnamon
2. 1-1/2 tbsp pumpkin pie spice
3. 15 oz can pumpkin
4. 14 oz can sweetened condensed milk
5. 2 beaten eggs
6. 1 unbaked pie shell
7. **Topping:** whipped cream

Preparation Method

1. Preheat your smoker to 325°F.
2. Place a baking sheet, rimmed, on the smoker upside down, or use a cake pan.
3. Combine all your ingredients in a bowl, large, except the pie shell then pour the mixture into a pie crust.
4. Place the pie on the baking sheet and smoke for about 50-60 minutes until a knife comes out clean when inserted. Make sure the center is set.
5. Remove and cool for about 2 hours or refrigerate overnight.
6. Serve with a whipped cream dollop and enjoy!

Nutritional Information

Calories 292, Total fat 11g, Saturated fat 5g, Total carbs 42g, Net carbs 40g, Protein 7g, Sugars 29g, Fiber 5g, Sodium 168mg, Potassium 329mg

Pellet-Grill Flatbread Pizza

This flatbread pizza comes out particularly good and flavorful. It is best served as a side dish or an appetizer.
Prep time: 10 minutes, **Cook time:** 20 minutes; **Serves** 3

Ingredients

- Dough
- 2 cups flour
- 1 tbsp salt
- 1 tbsp sugar
- 2 tbsp yeast
- 6 oz warm water
- Toppings
- Green/red bell pepper
- 1/2 garlic
- 1 zucchini

- 1/2 onion
- Olive oil
- 5 bacon strips
- 1 cup halved yellow cherry tomatoes
- Sliced jalapenos
- Sliced green olives
- Sliced kalamata olives
- Goat cheese
- **For drizzling:** Balsamic vinegar

Preparation Method

1. Combine all dough ingredients in a stand mixer bowl. Mix until the dough is smooth and elastic. Divide into 3 equal balls.
2. Roll each dough ball with a rolling pin into a thin round enough to fit a 12-inch skillet.
3. Grease the skillet using olive oil.
4. Meanwhile, turn your pellet grill on smoke for about 4-5 minutes with the lid open. Turn to high and preheat for about 10-15 minutes with the lid closed.
5. Once ready, arrange peppers, garlic, zucchini, and onion on the grill grate then drizzle with oil and salt. Check at 10 minutes.
6. Now remove zucchini from the grill and add bacon. Continue to cook for another 10 minutes until bacon is done.
7. Transfer the toppings on a chopping board to cool. Chop tomatoes, jalapenos and olive.
8. Brush your crust with oil and smash garlic with a fork over the crust. Smear carefully not to tear the crust.
9. Add toppings to the crust in the skillet.
10. Place the skillet on the grill and cook for about 20 minutes until brown edges.
11. Repeat for the other crusts.
12. Now drizzle each with vinegar and slice.
13. Serve and enjoy.

Nutritional Information

Calories 342, Total fat 1.2g, Saturated fat 0.2g, Total carbs 70.7g, Net carbs 66.8g, Protein 11.7g, Sugars 4.2g, Fiber 3.9g, Sodium 2333mg, Potassium 250mg

Grilled Nut Mix

The mixed nuts are sweetly seasoned with cayenne, brown sugar, thyme, and mustard powder. When Grilled, these nuts are very delicious leaving you carving for more.
Prep time: 15 minutes, **Cook time:** 20 minutes; **Serves** 8-12

Ingredients

- 3 cups mixed nuts (pecans, peanuts, almonds etc)
- 1/2 tbsp brown sugar
- 1 tbsp thyme, dried
- 1/4 tbsp mustard powder
- 1 tbsp olive oil, extra-virgin

Preparation Method

1. Preheat your pellet grill to 250°F with the lid closed for about 15 minutes.
2. Combine all ingredients in a bowl, large, then transfer into a cookie sheet lined with parchment paper.
3. Place the cookie sheet on a grill and grill for about 20 minutes.
4. Remove the nuts from the grill and let cool.
5. Serve and enjoy.

Nutritional Information

Calories 249, Total fat 21.5g, Saturated fat 3.5g, Total carbs 12.3g, Net carbs 10.1g, Protein 5.7g, Sugars 5.6g, Fiber 2.1g, Sodium 111mg, Potassium 205mg

Grilled Peaches and Cream

This is one of the easiest desserts to prepare at the comfort of your home. After grilling, drizzle with extra honey for perfection. Everyone in the family including your kids will love this.
Prep time: 15 minutes, **Cook time:** 8 minutes; **Serves** 8

Ingredients

- 4 halved and pitted peaches
- 1 tbsp vegetable oil
- 2 tbsp clover honey
- 1 cup cream cheese, soft with honey and nuts

Preparation Method

1. Preheat your pellet grill to medium-high heat.
2. Coat the peaches lightly with oil and place on the grill pit side down.
3. Grill for about 5 minutes until nice grill marks on the surfaces.

4. Turn over the peaches then drizzle with honey.
5. Spread and cream cheese dollop where the pit was and grill for additional 2-3 minutes until the filling becomes warm.
6. Serve immediately.

Nutritional Information

Calories 139, Total fat 10.2g, Saturated fat 5g, Total carbs 11.6g, Net carbs 11.6g, Protein 1.1g, Sugars 12g, Fiber 0g, Sodium 135mg, Potassium 19mg

Green Mountain Grill Chicken Flatbread

This recipe is so easy when prepared on a pellet grill bursting with flavor. Chicken flatbread is perfect for a weekend lunch or a weeknight dinner.
Prep time: 5 minutes, **Cook time:** 30 minutes; **Serves** 6

Ingredients

➢ 6 mini breads
➢ 1-1/2 cups divided buffalo sauce
➢ 4 cups cooked and cubed chicken breasts
➢ For drizzling: mozzarella cheese

Preparation Method

1. Preheat your pellet grill to 375 - 400°F.
2. Place the breads on a surface, flat, then evenly spread ½ cup buffalo sauce on all breads.
3. Toss together chicken breasts and 1 cup buffalo sauce then top over all the breads evenly.
4. Top each with mozzarella cheese.
5. Place the breads directly on the grill but over indirect heat. Close the lid.
6. Cook for about 5-7 minutes until slightly toasty edges, cheese is melted and fully hated chicken.
7. Remove and drizzle with ranch or blue cheese.
8. Enjoy!

Nutritional Information

Calories 346, Total fat 7.6g, Saturated fat 2g, Total Carbs 33.9g, Net Carbs 32.3g, Protein 32.5g, Sugars 0.8g, Fiber 1.6g, Sodium 642mg, Potassium 299mg

Grilled Homemade Croutons

These homemade croutons are golden brown and crispy adding wonderful texture when served with salads. They are easy and delicious and they just taste fabulous.
Prep time: 10 minutes, **Cook time:** 30 minutes; **Serves** 6

Ingredients

➢ 2 tbsp Mediterranean Blend Seasoning
➢ 1/4 cup olive oil
➢ 6 cups cubed bread

Preparation Method

1. Preheat your Green Mountain Grill to 250°F.
2. Combine seasoning and oil in a bowl then drizzle the mixture over the bread cubes. Toss to evenly coat.
3. Layer the bread cubes on a cookie sheet, large, and place on the grill.
4. Bake for about 30 minutes. Stir at intervals of 5 minutes for browning evenly.
5. Once dried out and golden brown, remove from the grill.
6. Serve and enjoy!

Nutritional Information

Calories 188, Total fat 10g, Saturated fat 2g, Total carbs 20g, Net carbs 19g, Protein 4g, Sugars 2g, Fiber 1g, Sodium 1716mg, Potassium 875mg

Grilled Cheddar Cheese

Grilled cheddar cheese brings back memories from Hickory farms of those crates that were crammed and shrink-wrapped full of Grilled cheese small rounds. You will enjoy it.
Prep time: 5 minutes, **Cook time:** 5 hour; **Serves** 2

Ingredients

➢ 2, 8-oz, cheddar cheese blocks

Preparation Method

1. Preheat and set your pellet grill to 90°F.
2. Place the cheese blocks directly on the grill grate and smoke for about 4 hours.
3. Remove and transfer into a plastic bag, resealable. Refrigerate for about 2 weeks to allow flavor from smoke to permeate your cheese.
4. Now enjoy!

Nutritional Information

Calories 115, Total fat 9.5g, Saturated fat 5.4g, Total carbs 0.9g, Net carbs 0.9g, Protein 6.5g, Sugars 0.1g, Fiber 0g, Sodium 185mg, Potassium 79mg

Grilled Mac and Cheese

This is a side dish that you never knew you needed but it will leave you yearning for more every time. Grilled mac and cheese is a recipe that your family will love great for weeknight meals and family barbeques.

Prep time: 2 minutes, **Cook time:** 1 hour; **Serves** 8

Ingredients

- 1/2 cup butter, salted
- 1/3 cup flour
- 1/2 tbsp salt
- 6 cups whole milk
- Dash of Worcestershire
- 1/2 tbsp dry mustard
- 1 lb small cooked shells, al dente in well-salted water
- 2 cups white cheddar, Grilled
- 2 cups cheddar jack cheese
- 1 cup crushed ritz

Preparation Method

1. Set your grill on "smoke" and run for about 5-10 minutes with the lid open until fire establishes. Now turn your grill to 325 °F then close the lid.
2. Melt butter in a saucepan, medium, over low--medium heat then whisk in flour.
3. Cook while whisking for about 5-6 minutes over low heat until light tan color.
4. Whisk in salt, milk, Worcestershire, and mustard over low-medium heat stirring frequently until a thickened sauce.
5. Stir noodles, small shells, white sauce, and 1 cup cheddar cheese in a large baking dish, 10x3" high-sided, coated with butter.
6. Top with 1 cup cheddar cheese and ritz.
7. Place on the grill and bake for about 25-30 minutes until a bubbly mixture and cheese melts.
8. Serve immediately. Enjoy!

Nutritional Information

Calories 628, Total fat 42g, Saturated fat 24g, Total carbs 38g, Net carbs 37g, Protein 25g, Sugars 11g, Fiber 1g, Sodium 807mg, Potassium 699mg

Berry Cobbler on a pellet grill

A Green Mountain Grill makes this berry cobbler recipe incredibly delicious. This will probably be your family's favorite dessert.
Prep time: 15 minutes, **Cook time:** 35 minutes; **Serves** 8

Ingredients

For fruit filling
- 3 cups frozen mixed berries
- 1 lemon juice
- 1 cup brown sugar
- 1 tbsp vanilla extract
- 1 tbsp lemon zest, finely grated
- A pinch of salt

For cobbler topping
- 1-1/2 cups all-purpose flour
- 1-1/2 tbsp baking powder
- 3 tbsp sugar, granulated
- 1/2 tbsp salt
- 8 tbsp cold butter
- 1/2 cup sour cream
- 2 tbsp raw sugar

Preparation Method

1. Set your pellet grill on "smoke" for about 4-5 minutes with the lid open until fire establishes and your grill starts smoking.
2. Preheat your grill to 350 °F for about 10-15 minutes with the grill lid closed.
3. Meanwhile, combine frozen mixed berries, Lemon juice, brown sugar, vanilla, lemon zest and pinch of salt. Transfer into a skillet and let the fruit sit and thaw.
4. Mix flour, baking powder, sugar, and salt in a bowl, medium. Cut cold butter into peas sizes using a pastry blender then add to the mixture. Stir to mix everything together.
5. Stir in sour cream until dough starts coming together.
6. Pinch small pieces of dough and place over the fruit until fully covered. Splash the top with raw sugar.
7. Now place the skillet directly on the grill grate, close the lid and cook for about 35 minutes until juices bubble, and a golden-brown dough topping.
8. Remove the skillet from the pellet grill and cool for several minutes.
9. Scoop and serve warm.

Nutritional Information

Calories 371, Total fat 13g, Saturated fat 8g, Total carbs 60g, Net carbs 58g, Protein 3g, Sugars 39g, Fiber 2g, Sodium 269mg, Potassium 123mg

Pellet Grill Apple Crisp

Looking for a crowd-pleaser dessert? Look no further This delicious apple crisp on your Green Mountain Grill is baked right and is topped using a crunchy, sweet, oat topping.
Prep time: 20 minutes, **Cook time:** 1 hour; **Serves** 15

Ingredients

Apples
➢ 10 large apples
➢ 1/2 cup flour
➢ 1 cup sugar, dark brown
➢ 1/2 tbsp cinnamon
➢ 1/2 cup butter slices

Crisp
➢ 3 cups oatmeal, old-fashioned
➢ 1-1/2 cups softened butter, salted
➢ 1-1/2 tbsp cinnamon
➢ 2 cups brown sugar

Preparation Method

1. Preheat your grill to 350 °F.
2. Wash, peel, core, and dice the apples into cubes, medium-size
3. Mix together flour, dark brown sugar, and cinnamon then toss with your apple cubes.
4. Spray a baking pan, 10x13", with cooking spray then place apples inside. Top with butter slices.
5. Mix all crisp ingredients in a medium bowl until well combined. Place the mixture over the apples.
6. Place on the grill and cook for about 1-hour checking after every 15-20 minutes to ensure cooking is even. Do not place it on the hottest grill part.
7. Remove and let sit for about 20-25 minutes
8. It's very warm.

Nutritional Information

Calories 528, Total fat 26g, Saturated fat 16g, Total carbs 75g, Net carbs 70g, Protein 4g, Sugars 51g, Fiber 5g, Sodium 209mg, Potassium 122mg

CHPTER 9

Grilled Tomato Cream Sauce

This is one of the juiciest and flavorful cream sauce recipes you will ever make. This Grilled tomato cream sauce sounds fancy but it is easy and one of the most delicious sauce ever.

Prep time: 15 minutes, **Cook time:** 1 hour 20 minutes; **Serves** 1

Ingredients

- 1 lb beefsteak tomatoes, fresh and quartered
- 1-1/2 tbsp olive oil
- Black pepper, freshly ground
- Salt, kosher
- 1/2 cup yellow onions, chopped
- 1 tbsp tomato paste
- 2 tbsp minced garlic
- Pinch cayenne
- 1/2 cup chicken stock
- 1/2 cup heavy cream

Preparation Method

1. Prepare your smoker using directions from the manufacturer.
2. Toss tomatoes and 1 tbsp oil in a bowl, mixing, then season with pepper and salt.
3. Smoke the tomatoes placed on a smoker rack for about 30 minutes. Remove and set aside reserving tomato juices.
4. Heat 1/2 tbsp oil in a saucepan over high-medium heat.
5. Add onion and cook for about 3-4 minutes. Add tomato paste and garlic then cook for an additional 1 minute.
6. Add Grilled tomatoes, cayenne, tomato juices, pepper, and salt then cook for about 3-4 minutes. Stir often.
7. Add chicken stock and boil for about 25-30 minutes under a gentle simmer. Stir often.
8. Place the mixture in a blender and puree until smooth. Now squeeze the mixture through a sieve, fine-mesh, to discard solids and release the juices,
9. Transfer the sauce in a saucepan, small, and add the cream.
10. Simmer for close to 6 minutes over low-medium heat until thickened slightly. Season with pepper and salt.
11. Serve warm with risotto cakes.

Nutritional Information

Calories 50, Total fat 5g, Saturated fat 1g, Total carbs 2g, Net carbs 2g, Protein 0g, Sugar 0g, Fiber 0g, Sodium: 69mg

Grilled Mushroom Sauce

Making mushroom sauce on a Green Mountain Grill is something you will love doing. It doesn't need much time to make and is much fun.
Prep time: 30 minutes, **Cook time:** 1 hour; **serves** 4

Ingredients

- 1-quart chef mix mushrooms
- 2 tbsp canola oil
- 1/4 cup julienned shallots
- 2 tbsp chopped garlic
- Salt and pepper to taste
- 1/4 cup alfasi cabernet sauvignon
- 1 cup beef stock
- 2 tbsp margarine

Preparation Method

1. Crumple four foil sheets into balls. Puncture multiple places in the foil pan then place mushrooms in the foil pan. Smoke in a pellet grill for about 30 minutes. Remove and cool.
2. Heat canola oil in a pan, sauté, add shallots and sauté until translucent.
3. Add mushrooms and cook until supple and rendered down.
4. Add garlic and season with pepper and salt. Cook until fragrant.
5. Add beef stock and wine then cook for about 6-8 minutes over low heat. Adjust seasoning.
6. Add margarine and stir until sauce is thickened and a nice sheen.
7. Serve and enjoy!

Nutritional Information

Calories 300, Total fat 30g, Saturated fat 2g, Total carbs 10g, Net carbs 10g, Protein 4g, Sugar 0g, Fiber 0g, Sodium: 514mg

Grilled Cranberry Sauce

Do you want to impress your guests? It is a very easy recipe to prepare and smoke adds flavor to the sauce. Don't wait to have this recipe for thanksgiving only.
Prep time: 10 minutes, **Cook time:** 1 hour; **Serves** 2

Ingredients

- 12 oz bag cranberries
- 2 chunks ginger, quartered
- 1 cup apple cider
- 1 tbsp honey whiskey
- 5.5 oz fruit juice
- 1/8 tbsp ground cloves
- 1/8 tbsp cinnamon
- 1/2 orange zest
- 1/2 orange
- 1 tbsp maple syrup
- 1 apple, diced and peeled
- 1/2 cup sugar

➢ 1/2 brown sugar

Preparation Method

1. Preheat your pellet grill to 375°F.
2. Place cranberries in a pan then add all other ingredients.
3. Place the pan on the grill and cook for about 1 hour until cooked through.
4. Remove ginger pieces and squeeze juices from the orange into tthe sauce.
5. Serve and enjoy!

Nutritional Information

Calories 48, Total fat 0.1g, Saturated fat 0g, Total carbs 12.3g, Net carbs 10g, Protein 0.4g, Sugar 7.5g, Fiber 2.3g, Sodium: 26mg

Grilled sriracha sauce

This sauce takes a little more time but once done they make one of the most flavorful sriracha.
Prep time: 10 minutes, **Cook time:** 1 hour; **serves** 2

Ingredients

➢ 1 lb Fresno chiles, stems pulled off and seeds removed
➢ 1/2 cup rice vinegar
➢ 1/2 cup red wine vinegar
➢ 1 carrot, medium and cut into rounds, 1/4 inch

➢ 1-1/2 tbsp sugar, dark-brown
➢ 4 garlic cloves, peeled
➢ 1 tbsp olive oil
➢ 1 tbsp kosher salt
➢ 1/2 cup water

Preparation Method

1. Smoke chiles in a smoker for about 15 minutes.
2. Bring to boil both vinegars then add carrots, sugar, and garlic. Simmer for about 15 minutes while covered. Cool for 30 minutes.
3. Place the chiles, olive oil, vinegar-vegetable mixture, salt, and ¼ cup water into a blender.
4. Blend for about 1-2 minutes on high. Add remaining water and blend again. You can add another 1/4 cup water if you want your sauce thinner.
5. Pour the sauce into jars and place in a refrigerator. Serve.

Nutritional Information

Calories 147, Total fat 5.23g, Saturated fat 0.7g, Total carbs 21g, Net carbs 18g, Protein 3g, Sugar 13g, Fiber 3g, Sodium: 671mg

Grilled soy sauce

This soy sauce is easy to make, fast, juicy, and very delicious. It is an excellent recipe that is perfect for pellet grill beginners which will soon make them feel confident in using pellet grill.

Prep time: 15 minutes, **Cook time:** 1 hour; **Serves** 1

Ingredients

- 100ml soy sauce
- Bradley flavor bisquettes cherry

Preparation Method

1. Put soy sauce in a heat-resistant bowl, large-mouth.
2. Smoke in a smoker at 158-176°F for about 1 hour. Stir a few times.
3. Remove and cool then put in a bottle. Let sit for one day.
4. Serve and enjoy!

Nutritional Information

Calories 110, Total fat 0g, Saturated fat 0g, Total carbs 25g, Net carbs 25g, Protein 2g, Sugar 25g, Fiber 0g, Sodium: 270mg

Grilled Garlic Sauce

Do you hate chaos and rush in getting meals ready? This recipe is absolutely the one for you. It is super easy, quick to cook, and delicious. Perfect for a summer night.

Prep time: 5 minutes, **Cook time:** 30 minutes; **Serves** 2

Ingredients

- 3 whole garlic heads
- 1/2 cup mayonnaise
- 1/4 cup sour cream
- 2 tbsp lemon juice
- 2 tbsp cider vinegar
- Salt to taste

Preparation Method

1. Cut the garlic heads off then place in a microwave-safe bowl, add 2 tbsp water and cover. Microwave for about 5-6 minutes on medium.
2. Heat your grill on medium.

3. Place the garlic heads in a shallow 'boat' foil and smoke for about 20-25 minutes until soft.
4. Transfer the garlic heads into a blender. Process for a few minutes until smooth.
5. Add remaining ingredients and process until everything is combined.
6. Enjoy!

Nutritional Information

Calories 20, Total fat 0g, Saturated fat 0g, Total carbs 10g, Net carbs 9g, Protein 0g, Sugar 0g, Fiber 1g, Sodium: 0mg

Grilled Cherry BBQ Sauce

Are you a fan of preparing own sauces? This recipe is a clear winner as the recipe is adaptable to your favorite tastes. Grilled cherry BBQ sauce is great with literally everything.
Prep time: 20 minutes, **Cook time:** 1 hour; **Serves** 2

Ingredients

1. 2 lb dark sweet cherries, pitted
2. 1 large chopped onion
3. 1/2 tbsp red pepper flakes, crushed
4. 1 tbsp kosher salt or to taste
5. 1/2 tbsp ginger, ground
6. 1/2 tbsp black pepper
7. 1/2 tbsp cumin
8. 1/2 tbsp cayenne pepper
9. 1 tbsp onion powder
10. 1 tbsp garlic powder
11. 1 tbsp Grilled paprika
12. 2 chopped garlic cloves
13. 1/2 cup pinot noir
14. 2 tbsp yellow mustard
15. 1-1/2 cups ketchup
16. 2 tbsp balsamic vinegar
17. 1/3 cup apple cider vinegar
18. 2 tbsp dark soy sauce
19. 1 tbsp liquid smoke
20. 1/4 cup Worcestershire sauce
21. 1 tbsp hatch chile powder
22. 3 tbsp honey
23. 1 cup brown sugar
24. 3 tbsp molasses

Preparation Method

1. Preheat your smoker to 250°F.
2. Place cherries in a baking dish, medium, and smoke for about 2 hours.
3. Saute onions and red pepper flakes in a pot, large, with 2 tbsp oil for about 4 minutes until softened.
4. Add salt and cook for an additional 1 minute.
5. Add ginger, black pepper, cumin, onion powder, garlic powder, and paprika then drizzle with oil and cook for about 1 minute until fragrant and spices bloom.
6. Stir in garlic and cook for about 30 seconds.
7. Pour in pinot noir scraping up for 1 minute for any bits stuck to your pan bottom.
8. Add yellow mustard, ketchup, balsamic vinegar, apple cider vinegar, dark soy sauce, liquid smoke, and Worcestershire sauce. Stir to combine.

9. Add cherries and simmer for about 10 minutes.
10. Add honey, brown sugar, and molasses and stir until combined. Simmer for about 30-45 minutes over low heat until your own liking.
11. Place everything into a blender and process until a smooth sauce.
12. Enjoy with favorite veggies or protein. You can refrigerate in jars for up to a month.

Nutritional Information

Calories 35, Total fat 0g, Saturated fat 0g, Total carbs 9g, Net carbs 9g, Protein 0g, Sugar 0g, Fiber 0g, Sodium: 0mg

Grilled Garlic White Sauce

A fancy way to serve sauce and impress your kids and all your guests. This Grilled Garlic White Sauce is perfect for the weekend and a recipe that many will be left yearning for more.
Prep time: 15 minutes, **Cook time:** 1 hour; **Serves** 2

Ingredients

➢ 2 cups hickory wood chips, soaked in water for 30 minutes
➢ 3 whole garlic heads
➢ 1/2 cup mayonnaise
➢ 1/3 cup sour cream
➢ 1 juiced lemon
➢ 2 tbsp apple cider vinegar
➢ Salt to taste

Preparation Method

1. Cut garlic heads to expose the inside and place in a container, microwave-safe, with 2 tbsp water. Microwave for about 5-6 minutes on medium.
2. Preheat your grill. Place garlic heads on a shallow foil "boat" and place it on the grill.
3. Close the grill and cook for about 20-25 minutes until soft completely. Remove and cool.
4. Transfer into a blender then add the remaining ingredients. Process until smooth.
5. Serve immediately or store in a refrigerator for up to 5 days.

Nutritional Information

Calories 20, Total fat 0g, Saturated fat 0g, Total carbs 8g, Net carbs 8g, Protein 0g, Sugar 0g, Fiber 0g, Sodium: 45mg

CHAPTER 11

A healthy 21-day Meal Plan

	LUNCH	SNACK	DINNER
1	Grilled Lamb chops	Grilled beef jerky	Grilled Midnight Brisket
2	Grilled Mushrooms	Grilled Chicken Kabobs	Butter Basted Porterhouse Steak
3	grilled shredded pork tacos	Teriyaki Beef Jerky	Grilled Chicken
4	Grilled Lamb Loin Chops	Barbecue Chicken wings	Wet-Rubbed St. Louis Ribs
5	grilled pork Chops	Spicy Candied Bacon	Cocoa Crusted Grilled Flank steak
6	Grilled Pulled Lamb Sliders	Cumin Lamb Skewers	Grilled Lamb Shoulder
7	Chicken Flatbread	Grilled Zucchini Squash Spears	Grilled Acorn Squash
8	Grilled Chicken	Lamb Meatballs	Grill Prime Rib Roast
9	chicken breasts	Grilled Deviled Eggs	Grill Spicy Sweet Potatoes
10	Grilled Vegetables	Grilled Carrot Dogs	pork crown Roast
11	Blackened Pork Chops	Grilled Bacon	Grilled Butter Basted Rib-eye
12	Grilled Asparagus	Bacon-wrapped Chicken Tenders	Grilled Buffalo Chicken Leg
13	Grilled Spicy Sweet Potatoes	Grilled Mexican Street Corn	Grilled Pork ribs
14	Togarashi Pork tenderloin	Barbecue Chicken wings	Supper Beef Roast
15	Grilled Lamb Shoulder	Pork Tenderloin Sliders	Crown rack of lamb
16	Grilled Cornish Hens	Grilled Stuffed Zucchini	Grilled Vegetables
17	Sheet pan Chicken Fajitas	Lamb Meatballs	Deli-style Roast beef
18	Pulled Pork	Grilled and fried chicken wings	Roasted Pork with Balsamic Strawberry Sauce
19	Grilled Mushrooms	Grilled Bacon	

20	Grilled Pork Ribs	Bacon Wrapped Jalapeno Poppers	Grilled Leg of Lamb
21	Grilled Lamb Chops	Grilled Deviled Eggs	Grilled Spatchcock Turkey

CONCLUSION

Although wood pellets grill isn't everyone's favorite choice, it's clear that a Green Mountain Grill is a must-have outdoor kitchen appliance. Whether you love smoking, grilling, roasting, barbecuing, or direct cooking of food, Green Mountain Grill is clearly versatile and has got you covered.

Cooking with a Green Mountain Grill allows you to choose the desired flavor of wood pellets to create the perfect smoke to flavor your food. Each wood pellet type has its personality and taste. The best part is you can use a single flavor or experiment with mixing and matching the flavors to invent your own combination.

Just like any cooking appliance, wood pellets have some drawbacks but the benefits overshadow them. It is therefore definitely worth a try.

Finally, while you will have fantastic smoking and grilling time with whichever Green Mountain Grill model you choose, the models are quite different. They hence offer different services and are suitable for different users. With new Green Mountain Grill series being produced each year, you need to shop smartly so that you buy a grill that perfectly fits you and meets all your needs.

APPENDIX: MEASUREMENT CONVERSION TABLE

DRY INGREDIENTS

dash	1/16 tablespoon
pinch	1/8 tablespoon
1 Tbsp	3 tablespoon
1/4 cup	4 Tbsp
1/3 cup	5 Tbsp+ 1 tbsp
1 cup	16 Tbsp
1 pint	2 cups
1 quart	2 pints
1 gallon	4 quarts

LIQUID INGREDIENTS

1Tbsp	1/2 fluid ounce
1 cup	6 fluid ounce
1 pint	16 fluid ounce
1 quart	32 fluid ounce
1 gallon	64 fluid ounce

CAPACITY AND VOLUME

1 tbsp	5 ml
1 Tbsp	15 ml
1 fl oz	30 ml
1/4 cup	59ml
1/3 cup	79ml
1 cup	236
1 pint	473
1 quart	950ml
1 gallon	3.8 ltrs
Weight and mass	
1 ouce	28 grams
1/4 lb	113 grams
1 lb	454 grams

VOLUME AND CAPACITY

1 ml	1/5 tbsp
5 ml	1 tbsp
15 ml	1 Tbsp
30ml	1 fl oz
50 ml	1/5 cup
100ml	3.4 fl oz
240ml	1 cup
1 ltr	1.6 quarts
Mass and weight	
1 gram	0.035oz
100g	3.5 oz
500g	1.1 lb
1 kl	2.205lb

TEMPERATURE CONVERSION

250°F	120°C
275°F	135°C
300°F	150°C
325°F	163°C
350°F	177°C
375°F	190°C
400°F	204°C
425°F	220°C
450°F	232°C
475°F	246°C
500°F	260°C